Also by Tucker Carlson

Ship of Fools

THE
LONG SLIDE

Thirty Years in American Journalism

TUCKER CARLSON

THRESHOLD EDITIONS
New York London Toronto Sydney New Delhi

Threshold Editions
An Imprint of Simon & Schuster, Inc.
1230 Avenue of the Americas
New York, NY 10020

First Threshold Editions hardcover edition August 2021

THRESHOLD EDITIONS and colophon are trademarks of Simon & Schuster, Inc.

For information about special discounts for bulk purchases, please contact Simon & Schuster Special Sales at 1-866-506-1949 or business@simonandschuster.com.

The Simon & Schuster Speakers Bureau can bring authors to your live event. For more information, or to book an event, contact the Simon & Schuster Speakers Bureau at 1-866-248-3049 or visit our website at www.simonspeakers.com.

Interior design by Davina Mock

Manufactured in the United States of America

10 9 8 7 6 5 4 3 2 1

Library of Congress Cataloging-in-Publication Data

ISBN 978-1-5011-8369-0
ISBN 978-1-5011-8371-3 (ebook)

To Susie

CONTENTS

CONTENTS

ACKNOWLEDGMENT

I'd like to acknowledge Jonathan Karp of Simon & Schuster, whose descent from open-minded book editor to cartoonish corporate censor mirrors the decline of America itself. It's been a sad education watching it happen.

INTRODUCTION

This is a collection of magazine stories. I had second thoughts about publishing it. Like takeout Chinese food, journalism is meant to be consumed immediately. The longer it sits around, the less appealing it becomes. You wouldn't want to reheat the lo mein you bought twenty-five years ago.

But in this case, I'm glad I did. Magazine journalism is worth remembering. They're mostly gone now, but for a long time magazines played a significant role in the life of the country. I grew up in a smallish town thirty miles from the Mexican border. Our neighbors were generally affluent and well educated, but the place still felt isolated. Every week, bundles of magazines arrived at our house, describing the world beyond La Jolla: *Time, National Geographic, U.S. News & World Report, The American Spectator, Boy's Life, Commentary, National Lam-*

poon, Soldier of Fortune. I read every one of them. If you wanted perspective, there was no choice. Our local newspaper was thin. The internet didn't exist. On TV, there were game shows, *Fantasy Island*, and *Love Boat*. After school, we watched reruns of *The Brady Bunch*. If you wanted to understand what the rest of the world was like, you read magazines.

My first employment out of college was as assistant editor of a quarterly magazine. I fact-checked features over the phone for $14,000 a year. I was thrilled to have the job. I was even happier to write for the magazine, and subsequently many others. I wrote magazine stories for decades, long after I went into television and no longer needed the $600. I did it because it was interesting. In order to produce a decent magazine piece, you had to go places, meet people, see unusual things. It was an adventure every time.

What do all those magazine stories look like years later? Reading your own journalism is like finding your diary from high school. It makes you blush. Could I really have been that naive and self-important? Yep. And nasty, too. I once wrote a profile of William Cohen, who for a time was Bill Clinton's secretary of defense. Cohen wasn't an especially commanding figure, but he was an awfully nice man. You could sense that the moment you met him. Why did I feel the need to mock the syrupy poetry he'd written about his first wife? I can't remember now. I wish I hadn't.

Even more distressing is how insignificant many of the subjects I wrote about look in retrospect. I spent months covering Senator Bob Dole's run for president. I traveled on Dole's plane, jockeyed to interview him, followed him across the country like a teenaged Led Zeppelin groupie. In 1996, Bob Dole was a big deal. It's hard now to understand why.

That's true for so many people I covered. We thought they were important. Now they're forgotten. A surprising number of them are dead, though I guess that shouldn't be surprising. Death and irrelevance are coming for all of us. That's the one certain thing. Repeat that to yourself every morning, and things fall into perspective. Most of what we think matters really doesn't.

One exception to this is the state of the country. That does matter. And after wading through more than 100,000 words of old journalism, I can report that our country has changed. It's more crowded, for one thing. The American population has grown by close to 100 million people since I started in the business. Technology has grown apace, of course, transforming everyone and everything. On my first day as a professional journalist, I'd never heard of the internet. I'd never even used a computer. Now I rarely see my coworkers in person. Daily life exists online.

But it's the changes in attitudes that strike me most. In 1991, journalists were proud to be open-minded, and I was proud to become one. My father was a reporter, and he embodied everything I associated with journalism. He was smart, curious, and relentlessly skeptical. It was impossible to bullshit my father. My brother and I never even tried. Above all, he was brave. If he thought something was true, he felt free to say it. "Truth is a defense," he often said. This is America. You're allowed to be honest.

That could have been the motto of every magazine I ever worked for, liberal or conservative. Editors saw themselves as the guardians of free speech and unfettered inquiry. That was their job. If the people they exposed to public ridicule didn't like it, tough. The complaints of the guilty were a badge of honor. Editors posted hate mail on bulletin boards in the newsroom. Being despised was something you bragged about. It meant you were telling the truth.

Over in corporate America—at IBM or GE or Exxon— managers told their drones what they were allowed to say in public. There were no rules like that in journalism. No one told journalists what to say. Reporters were free men, and they lived like it. If they could prove it, they could write it. Period. That was the whole point of belonging to a class specifically protected by the Bill of Rights.

In 1994, Richard Herrnstein and Charles Murray published *The Bell Curve,* a book that included a chapter about racial differences in IQ. Many people were offended by *The Bell Curve,* including many liberal reporters. Yet nobody in mainstream journalism tried to censor the book. CNN didn't pressure retailers not to sell *The Bell Curve.* The *New York Times* didn't demand that its authors lose their jobs. Instead, journalists debated the facts and ideas in the book. *The New Republic* devoted an entire issue to *The Bell Curve,* and let its writers and editors weigh in with their views. Not all of them had the same opinions. That was okay. Nobody got fired for disagreeing with the majority.

The New Republic was always liberal, but at the time it was still a magazine. It produced journalism, not just propaganda. I had plenty of friends who worked there. A couple of times, I wrote for it myself, including a story that's included in this book. In the fall of 2007, *The New Republic* sent me to Nevada to cover Texas congressman Ron Paul, who was running for president. Paul was a highly eccentric person, as you'll see in the piece, but in the end I decided I liked him. He was completely sincere, a quality we undervalue in Washington, probably because we so rarely see it.

Others at *The New Republic* despised Ron Paul. They believed he was a menace to the country. They were particularly offended by Paul's isolationist foreign policy views, which contradicted everything *The New Republic* had been saying for decades in editorials. A month later, a *New Republic* reporter called Jamie Kirchick responded to my piece by attacking Ron Paul in a long diatribe that dismissed him as a bigoted lunatic. That was fine with me. Jamie Kirchick had one view of Ron Paul; I had another. Both of us were allowed to express what we thought. What mattered to me was that a fervently neoconservative magazine had allowed me to write an affectionate, evenhanded story about a guy who opposed neoconservatives. That seemed like honorable journalism.

None of this was unusual at the time. As ideological as some of the writers at *The New Republic* were, most of them felt obligated to work toward some state of open-mindedness. They regarded themselves as journalists, not activists. My editors there understood that I usually didn't agree with their politics. That wasn't a problem. Politics wasn't everything.

Today, politics is everything. There's no chance *The New Republic* would ever again publish one of my stories. Editors at *The New Republic* no longer encourage dissent or praise free thinking. They penalize it. They don't facilitate important national conversations. They end them. *The New Republic* has become close-minded and reflexively partisan, exactly the qualities it once hated.

It's been awful to watch this happen, but it's no longer surprising. Censorship is now the rule in popular media; news outlets openly censor ideas they don't like, and encourage others to do the same. Journalism has been utterly corrupted. Yet somehow I never thought I'd see the same variety of rot in book publishing. To a greater degree even than reporters, book publishers always described themselves as defenders of open and rational debates about ideas. The people who edited books believed they were curators of the country's intellectual life. For that reason, over the course of a century, they relentlessly fought any form of censorship.

When Margaret Sanger was convicted of a crime in 1915 for sending birth control literature thorough the mail, book publishers defended her. When the state of Tennessee banned Charles Darwin's *On the Origin of Species* because it contradicted the creation story in Genesis, publishers rose in support of Darwin and of science itself. When censors tried to suppress Mark Twain and Walt Whitman and D. H. Lawrence and countless other authors who'd been deemed "controversial" by some interest group or other, the American publishing establishment promoted them. Publishers supported Banned Books

Week and the Freedom to Read Foundation. Americans should be able to read whatever books they want, publishers told us, but they should start with the books the authorities have tried to suppress. As they often said, there's only one answer to offensive speech, and it's more speech. They said this a lot. It seemed like they meant it.

At some point, they stopped meaning it. In December 2016, Simon & Schuster, one of the largest and oldest publishers in the country, signed a book deal with Milo Yiannopoulos. Yiannopoulos was an editor at Breitbart News. He was exuberantly gay, wildly articulate, and unapologetically right-wing. Media outlets dismissed him as a "provocateur." Journalists suggested that Yiannopoulos's habit of questioning dominant cultural clichés was somehow immoral.

This was strange to see. In Yiannopoulos's case, the normal rules seemed inverted: Yiannopoulos was funny and outrageous, but for the first time in memory, fashionable people considered that bad. When entertainers like Kathy Griffin or Sarah Silverman made lame jokes designed to affirm the professional class's sense of its own moral superiority, they were praised as daring, for "pushing boundaries." Yiannopoulos was wittier than either one of them, but he pushed real boundaries. None of our taste-makers congratulated him for it. Many of them became hysterical.

The *Chicago Review of Books* denounced Simon & Schuster's contract with Yiannopoulos as a "disgusting validation of hate," and announced that going forward, they would no longer review any book the company published. Roxane Gay, a forgettable activist type from Yale, pulled her own forgettable activist-type book from Simon & Schuster in protest. Gay couldn't bear the moral stain of being in the same catalog as Milo Yiannopoulos.

Attacks like these rattled Simon & Schuster, as well as its corporate parent, CBS. Les Moonves, who was then running CBS, had a conversation with Simon & Schuster executives about what to do next. According to one participant in that call, the group decided to "water the book down to the point that Milo wouldn't want to publish it." In other words, they planned to euthanize the project in editing.

None of Yiannopoulos's many fans outside of publishing knew this was going on, or seemed deterred by the public controversies over him. So many people pre-ordered copies of his book online that it became a bestseller before it was published.

In the end, commercial success wasn't enough to save Yiannopoulos's book. In February 2017, Simon & Schuster issued a statement announcing they'd canceled it. Amazon immediately eliminated the listing. The pretext for the cancellation was an interview that Yiannopoulos had given, more a year before, to a podcast called *Drunken Peasants*. Press accounts explained that during a conversation about sex abuse in the Catholic Church, Yiannopoulos had "endorsed pedophilia." No large media outlet printed the full transcript of the interview. Readers were left with the impression that Yiannopoulos had come out in favor of child molestation. Here's what Yiannopoulos actually said:

"The law [determining the legal age of sexual consent] is probably about right. That's probably roughly the right age. I think it's probably about okay, but there are certainly people who are capable of giving consent at a younger age. I certainly consider myself to be one of them, people who are sexually active younger. I think it particularly happens in the gay world, by the way. In many cases, actually those relationships with older men—this is one reason I hate the left. This stupid one size fits all policing of culture. This sort of arbitrary and oppressive idea of consent, which totally destroys, you know, the understanding that many of us have—the complexities and subtleties and complicated nature of many relationships. You know, people are messy and complex. In the homosexual world particularly. Some of those relationships between younger boys and older men, the sort of coming-of-age relationships, the relationships in which those older men help those young boys to discover who they are, and give them security and safety, and provide them with love and a reliable sort of a rock [in cases where] where they can't speak to their parents."

Yiannopoulos went on to say that he himself had been molested by a Catholic priest. Clearly he'd thought a lot about the topic. You might be offended by Yiannopoulos's views on gay sex. But was he, as Paul Farhi of the *Washington Post* claimed, "endorsing pedophilia"? No. He wasn't. So why did Simon & Schuster cancel him?

As it happens, I was working on a book for Simon & Schuster at roughly this time. The editor assigned to my book had been Yiannopoulos's editor, Mitchell Ivers. At breakfast one morning in New York, I asked Ivers why the company had killed Yiannopoulos's book. The question clearly made him uncomfortable, but because Ivers wasn't the executive who'd made the decision, I didn't press him. But I was struck by the fact that in his answer, Ivers never mentioned Yiannopoulos's infamous podcast. "Endorsing pedophilia" didn't seem to be the real reason the book was killed.

Could Simon & Schuster really have canceled such a promising book because the author's political opponents had complained about it? That seemed impossible to me. It would amount to such a grotesque violation of every principle American book publishing had claimed to support for the last hundred years that I couldn't digest it. I assumed something else must have happened between Yiannopoulos and Simon & Schuster, something I didn't know about.

I assumed that for almost four years. Then, in the early summer of 2020, George Floyd died in the street outside a convenience store in Minneapolis. Anger over Floyd's death swiftly grew into a nationwide protest. The BLM-led movement that resulted spawned riots, forced wholesale changes to the curricula in schools, and in the end led to a reordering of priorities in many Americans companies—including, as it turned out, Simon & Schuster.

Barely a month after George Floyd's death, Simon & Schuster hired a new publisher called Dana Canedy. Canedy was a former newspaper reporter, who'd most recently worked as the administrator of the Pulitzer Prizes. "Meet Dana Canedy, the first black publisher of a major imprint"—that was the headline on CNBC the day she started. That theme was echoed on many other news sites: Dana Canedy, diversity pioneer. Less prominently noted was the fact that Dana Canedy had zero experience in book publishing. She hadn't spent a single day in the business before getting the top job.

Canedy seemed aware that others might notice this. In an interview with the *New York Times,* she described the moment in which she was hired as "an era of racial reckoning." Jonathan Karp, the chief executive at Simon & Schuster, explained his thinking about Canedy this way: "I wanted somebody who was going to be a magnet for the best talent."

But magnets don't just attract. They also repel. Almost immediately after Canedy started at Simons & Schuster, Threshold Editions passed on a second book from the conservative author Candace Owens. From a business perspective, it was a puzzling move. Owens's previous book, called *Blackout,* had been a *New York Times* bestseller. The book had been all over conservative media, and attracted more than 15,000 positive ratings on Amazon. Owens had become one of the biggest draws in nonfiction publishing in America. By any definition, Candace Owens qualified as "the best talent." Suddenly, Simon & Schuster didn't want her.

Why would a publisher turn down an all-but-guaranteed bestseller? When the *New York Times* reported that Simon & Schuster planned to "stop publishing" Owens, I texted Jonathan Karp to find out. "Is it true?" I asked. It seemed like a straightforward question. I couldn't get a straightforward answer.

"I think another company is publishing Candace Owens," Karp replied, "but you'd have to confirm that with her. I never met her or interacted with her."

As our exchange lengthened, Karp conceded that Simon & Schuster did not have "a deal to publish the next book by Candace Owens." But why was that? Owens had been working on another proposal for Simon & Schuster. Her first book sold extraordinarily well. Why not publish the next book?

"That's between the author and the publisher," Karp replied. "We're not going to comment."

That turned out to be a flexible standard, as Josh Hawley soon discovered. Hawley was a first-term Republican senator from Missouri. He was one of the rare anti-corporate voices in a party that has long taken its direction from the Chamber of Commerce. Just after Christmas of 2020, Hawley was finishing a book for Simon & Schuster about the threat that Silicon Valley tech monopolies pose to American life. The book had already been widely promoted in the media. Simon & Schuster seemed thrilled with it.

On December 29, Jonathan Karp emailed Hawley to say he'd just read the first nine chapters. Karp's assessment: "They are excellent! The writing is clear, commanding, and persuasive." Karp described Hawley's book as "lively and relevant." He called Hawley's attack on Facebook "a powerful critique."

A week later, on January 5, 2021, Hawley got an email from his editor at Simon & Schuster, Natasha Simons. By this point, Hawley had already announced that he planned to cast what was already the most criticized vote of his life, against certifying the presidential election results in the state of Pennsylvania. Hawley wanted several outstanding questions about election integrity investigated before the vote was certified. Objectively, that didn't seem like an outrageous request. There was certainly precedent for it. Democrats in Congress had voted against certifying the vote in states after previous elections, including after the 2016 race. In 2005, 31 House Democrats voted against certifying George W. Bush's victory.

If they'd been following the news about one of their own authors, executives at Simon & Schuster would have known that Hawley planned to vote against election certification in Pennsylvania. No one objected. "Hi, Senator Hawley," wrote editor Natasha Simons in a note. "You have had quite a few newsworthy weeks! I want to thank you for all the fighting you're doing for the American people and the dignity and graciousness with which you're going it. I'm very glad we have you in the arena." Simons explained that she was eager to get Hawley's manuscript edited, "so we can begin the official book making process and keep all on track for a June publication." She ended with no hint of what lay ahead: "Thanks and happy new year!"

The next day, everything changed. On January 6, a group of Trump supporters walked from a political rally in downtown Washington to the U.S. Capitol. As cameras rolled, they fought with police, burst through the doors of the building, and wandered around freely inside. Hundreds of them were later arrested by federal law enforcement; many were held without bail for months. No one in public life defended what happened. Every member of Congress denounced it.

Hawley released his statement immediately: "Thank you to the brave law enforcement officials who have put their lives on the line," he wrote at 4:26 p.m. that day. "The violence must end, those who attacked police and broke the law must be prosecuted, and Congress must get back to work and finish its job."

None of Hawley's behavior on January 6 seemed especially controversial. Hawley had done nothing to encourage rioting, at the Capitol or anywhere else. The moment a riot occurred, he called for an end to violence, praised the Capitol Police, and demanded the rioters be arrested and charged. These were hardly the words of an insurrectionist.

The next day, Simon & Schuster canceled his book. "After witnessing the disturbing, deadly insurrection that took place on Wednesday in Washington, D.C.," the company said in a statement that was reprinted around the world, "Simon & Schuster has decided to cancel publication of Senator Josh Hawley's forthcoming book." Jonathan Karp may have pledged not to "comment on author relationships," but the statement was specific about why the company made the decision. Because "we take seriously our larger public responsibility as citizens," Simon & Schuster's executives explained, we "cannot support Senator Hawley after his role in what became a dangerous threat to our democracy and freedom."

The result was politically devastating to Josh Hawley. His partisan opponents claimed that Hawley was responsible for the violence at the Capitol. His own book publisher agreed with them. Instantly, Hawley became one of the most reviled people in Washington.

But the question remained: what, specifically, had Josh Hawley done wrong? What was his crime? Hawley cast a vote, consistent with recent precedent, that his political opponents didn't like. That's hardly unplowed ground in the United States Senate. It happens every day. By doing what senators so often do, how did Hawley play a "role" in a "dangerous threat to our democracy and freedom." What was his role? I couldn't stop wondering about this. A few days later, I called Jonathan Karp and Dana Canedy at Simon & Schuster to find out. We spoke over Zoom for nearly an hour. It was a revealing conversation.

Canedy began by explaining that she'd made the decision to cancel Josh Hawley's book as a business executive, with no reference to her own politics. "Any personal views I may or may not have had were completely irrelevant," she explained. "I'm a journalist, so I'm used to creating distance in situations and trying to think without putting any emotion or point of view in." After deciding to kill Josh Hawley's contract, Canedy recalled that "a calm came over me and I was at peace with it."

But if Canedy felt such peace, why did she then attack Hawley in a press release? She seemed wounded by the question. An attack? Sending a statement to the *New York Times* accusing a man of participating in a "dangerous threat to our democracy and freedom" was in no way an attack on anyone, least of all Josh Hawley, Canedy explained. "I'm not somebody who does attacks. Jon [Karp] certainly isn't. That's not our character."

Character? A debate about the personal moral qualities of publishing executives seemed like a conversational cul-de-sac, so I switched tacks and once again asked what Josh Hawley had done wrong. What was his crime? Canedy replied that Hawley had "participated in a way that would bring lots of scorn upon him."

How so? I asked.

"If you're asking me what he did," Canedy replied, "we know what he did." But I sincerely didn't know.

At this point, Jonathan Karp interjected. The problem, Karp said, was one of hypocrisy. Hawley's book had been titled *The Tyranny of Big Tech*. And yet, "we thought that he had a role in tyranny—the tyranny that occurred at the Capitol. He had a role in it by supporting the challenge" to Pennsylvania's election results.

So a vote in the Senate that some people don't like is now "tyranny"? Yes, Karp replied. And not just that. "Also his inability to apologize or make any kind of statement after the attack. That indicated a problem with his judgement." Karp seemed unaware that Hawley had issued a statement condemning the riot on the afternoon of January 6, immediately after it happened.

I didn't bother to correct him, because at this point, both Karp and Canedy seemed to lose interest in discussing the details of the day, or of the days that preceded it. Neither seemed to know precisely what had happened, or to care.

Instead they intensified their use of the word "scorn," as if that explained everything: Hawley had "opened himself up to scorn," Karp said. Josh Hawley was "widely scorned by people for the actions that he took," Canedy explained. Finally, Canedy summed it up this way: "What we did ultimately decide is that those actions brought so much scorn."

Scorn from whom? That seemed like an important question. I asked it again. Canedy went first. After the riot, she said, other members of Congress were "trying to reconcile folks to get the country, to get the Senate and the Congress, back on track to do the people's work." But not Josh Hawley. Hawley, she said, "still pressed on" with his concerns about the election.

That didn't strike me as unusual behavior in Washington, so I asked once again who was offended by the sight of partisanship in the Senate, and why? Canedy didn't answer directly. Instead she noted that, when Josh Hawley continued to talk about the presidential election, "people like his newspaper and his donor and his mentor all thought this was a bridge too far into contributing to the tyranny of the day."

The tyranny of the day?

Yes, she said. "There was scorn there." Some, she said, had even called for Josh Hawley to resign.

Like who?

"The truth is," Canedy replied, "off the top of my head, I can't name the folks who are calling for him to resign, but there are. If you want that, it's easy enough to have your researchers google."

At this point, Karp went to his notes. "I want to read you something," he said. "Let me just read you this paragraph, because it does encapsulate our view. It was written by Ron Charles, who's a really good book reviewer in the *Washington Post*: 'The Senator must know that Simon & Schuster didn't cancel his contract because he was representing his constituents. The company cancelled his contract because he's become a symbol of violent extremism and toxic deception that no self-respecting private company wants to promote. That's not a direct assault on the first amendment. That's a direct exercise of free enterprise."

Karp let the words hang in the air for a moment. "I agree with that," he said.

I pondered this. So a guy who works at the *Washington Post*, a newspaper owned by the richest man in the world, has declared that Senator Josh Hawley of Missouri is "a symbol of violent extremism." No one's claiming that Hawley is a practitioner of violent extremism, or even an organizer of violent extremism. But for reasons that nobody can or will explain, Josh Hawley has now been designated a "symbol" of violent extremism, and for that reason alone, one of the largest publishers in the world was correct to cancel Hawley's book about why big media companies are a threat to speech.

This seemed like a worrisome standard to me—not to mention unintentionally hilarious—and I said so. "You can see why this would make people who believe in free expression and the intellectual life of the country nervous, can't you?" I asked.

"No," said Canedy, "I can't. I actually can't."

Karp piped up: "It is a business decision, Tucker." So, in fact, it had nothing to do with the moral crime of becoming a symbol of violent extremism. This was purely about business. Josh Hawley had been criticized by powerful people. Simon & Schuster had concluded that criticism would hurt the book's chances in the marketplace. It was that simple.

As Canedy put it, "we think that he brought a lot of scorn on himself with this thing at the time when he's turning in this book. That made us think, hmm, from a business point of view, maybe this is not what we need to be doing right now."

As a "business decision," Simon & Schuster's strategy didn't make sense. How well do policy books from U.S. senators typically sell? Not very well. Would a nationwide controversy increase or decrease sales of a book like that? Does controversy generate retail interest? Do partisan passions motivate book buying? These are rhetorical questions. Every best-selling political author is reviled by large numbers of people. Every single one. This is a divided country. If one side hate hates you, the other side buys your books. There isn't a marketing director in the country who doesn't know that. The explanation was absurd.

But once again, it did raise interesting questions. For example, on what grounds can private companies decide not to do business with individuals? For Dana Canedy, the answer was simple: "publishers have a right to decide who they will and will not publish," she said. Period.

Okay. So if that's the standard, do restaurants have the right to decide whom eats in them? I asked.

"No, of course not," Canedy snapped.

Got it. Massive publishing conglomerates have the right to choose whom they do business with. Tiny, family-owned diners do not?

Canedy paused. Actually, she replied, sometimes diner owners do. In those cases in which a patron in a restaurant is "doing something that's going to hurt that business, they have an absolute right not to serve that person for sure."

Fair enough. But how exactly did this standard apply to Josh Hawley? Hawley didn't "do" anything to hurt Simon & Schuster. Hawley cast the same vote that dozens of Democrats in Congress had cast in elections past. His book contract didn't prohibit him from casting that vote. News outlets reported that he planned to cast it, but no one at Simon & Schuster complained to Hawley. Hawley's editor praised him for it. "I want to thank you for all the fighting you're doing for the American people," she wrote.

So why did Simon & Schuster cancel Josh Hawley's book, and then suggest he was a "dangerous threat to our democracy and freedom"? Because a group of angry partisans demanded that Simon & Schuster do that. That was the only reason.

Consider, I said to Karp and Canedy, how that same principle might work in a restaurant. A group of people decides that you shouldn't be allowed to eat at, say, a lunch counter. They don't like what you stand for, or how you look. So they yell at you and call you names. They threaten to hurt the restaurant's revenues if the restaurant takes your business. In the face of the mob, the restaurant caves, and denies you service. Is that okay?

Dana Canedy didn't like the analogy at all. She sounded highly annoyed, and accused me of using "outrageous hypotheticals." That made me laugh, considering there was nothing hypothetical about it. That very scenario played out many times over decades in the American South, as Canedy of course well knew.

At this point, Karp swooped in to save her. "You're a really good debater," he said, as if the whole line of questioning had been some kind of spooky magic trick, rhetorical three-card monte I'd used to fool them and make them look stupid. All those big words. "You're a really good debater."

Before we hung up, Karp tried one last time to convince me that there was nothing at all political about the way the company had treated Josh Hawley. Simon & Schuster isn't partisan, Karp assured. "We published Candace Owens last year."

The next day, Karp sent me a long email letting me know how much he'd appreciated my "efforts to understand our rationale on canceling Senator Hawley's book." But he was concerned, he said, about whether he and Dana Canedy had "sufficiently answered" the questions I'd asked. My main question all along had been simple: how exactly was Josh Hawley's vote in the Senate responsible for a riot? Even in an email, Karp couldn't answer it.

Karp included a lot of emphatic adjectives, combined with partisan assumptions posing as established facts. At one point, he described the 2020 contest as being "widely deemed a free and fair election," as if that was true or meant anything. He mentioned that a liberal newspaper in Missouri didn't like Josh Hawley, and by the way, neither did that *Washington Post* book reviewer he'd told me about before. Karp included the guy's line about how Hawley had "become a symbol of violent extremism," in case I'd missed it the first time.

All of this, Karp wrote, proved that Senator Josh Hawley had "brought opprobrium of an unprecedented level upon himself and, by association, Simon & Schuster, and we made the determination not to go forward with the book."

At the end of the email, once again and hilariously, Karp reminded me that Simon & Schuster had published a book by Candace Owens. I don't think I've ever been more amused.

A couple of weeks later, I learned about the internal pressure Simon & Schuster had faced to cancel Hawley's book. A group of nearly six hundred self-described "publishing professionals" signed an open letter demanding that no person like Josh Hawley ever receive a book contract again. As they put it, "no one who incited, suborned, instigated, or otherwise supported the January 6, 2021, coup attempt should have their philosophies remunerated and disseminated through our beloved publishing houses."

This ban, the signatories wrote, must apply to all former Trump administration employees as well: "participation in the administration of Donald Trump must be considered a uniquely mitigating criterion for publishing houses when considering book deals. . . . No participant in an administration that caged children, performed involuntary surgeries on captive women, and scoffed at science as millions were infected with a deadly virus should be enriched by the almost rote largesse of a big book deal."

Preventing Republicans from writing books, the group explained, was a moral imperative, but it was also a legal requirement. The letter cited "Son of Sam" laws, which "exist to prevent criminals from benefiting financially from writing about their crimes. In that spirit, those who enabled, promulgated, and covered up crimes against the American people should not be enriched through the coffers of publishing."

The publishing professionals ended on a militant note. They were tired, they said, "of the industry we love enriching the monsters among us, and we will do whatever is in our power to stop it." Included among the signatories were a number of Simon & Schuster employees. At least one of them claimed to have worked on Josh Hawley's book.

Now that Donald Trump is gone, Simon & Schuster clearly intends to have much warmer relations with America's political leaders. Just two weeks after Joe Biden's inauguration, the company announced it planned to publish a memoir by Biden's son, Hunter. The book was called *Beautiful Things*.

The militant "publishing professionals" didn't write an outraged letter objecting to the project. Their standards had changed overnight. Like Josh Hawley, Hunter Biden had been accused by his political opponents of committing crimes. Unlike Josh Hawley, Biden was, at the very moment he signed the Simon & Schuster deal, the subject of an active criminal investigation by the Justice Department. The FBI was investigating Biden's business dealings in China.

Yet somehow a federal criminal investigation was not a disqualifying problem, either for the inflamed publishing professional community, or for Hunter Biden. Apparently, Son of Sam laws don't apply to the sons of Democratic presidents. Simon & Schuster didn't cancel the book in an angry press release, but instead promoted it enthusiastically. The excerpt the company sent to media outlets could have been torn from the jacket of a romance novel: "I come from a family forged by tragedies and bound by a remarkable, unbreakable love," it read.

The Biden family's "remarkable, unbreakable love"—that was a story line that evoked no scorn whatsoever at Simon & Schuster. According to news reports, the company paid Hunter Biden about $2 million for telling it. Readers were less enthusiastic. The book never cracked the top ten on the best-seller list.

The fact that Hunter Biden got rich from a mediocre book didn't bother or surprise me. As it happened, I knew Hunter fairly well. For years we lived near each other in Washington, and sometimes had dinner. He always struck me as a screwed-up guy who was trying to do the right thing most of the time, but could never really beat his drug problem. I didn't consider Hunter a bad person, or for that matter even politically liberal. He understood the Democratic Party in nonideological terms, as a family business. His entire life had been defined by his father's job. He got into Yale Law School on the strength of his last name, and made a living on it for decades after. I wasn't shocked when Simon & Schuster signed him. That's how things work in a country that no longer makes any pretense of being a meritocracy.

What did shock me was the contrast between the way Simon & Schuster executives treated Hunter, and the way they treated Josh Hawley. The difference couldn't have been starker. Jonathan Karp disliked Hawley's opinions and his political party. He approved of Hunter's. So under pressure from partisans, Simon & Schuster canceled one and promoted the other. None of this was the result of any ethical consideration. It had little to do with book sales. It was political.

This seemed like a new and ominous standard. I considered

all the magazine pieces I'd written over the years for editors who passionately disagreed with my politics—most of them, probably. It never once occurred to me that a story of mine might be killed, or rewritten into mush, because some executive thought I'd voted the wrong way. If small-minded partisans had been in charge, I never could have stayed in the business. As this point, people with my opinions can't. They've been driven from traditional journalism.

That's what I thought about as I reread the pieces that follow. Not only were they written a long time ago, but many of them couldn't be written today. Enjoy the time capsule.

———————

In the summer of 2003, I flew to West Africa with Al Sharpton, Cornel West, and members of the Nation of Islam. The point of the trip, purportedly, was to stop the civil war that was then destroying Liberia. I was in favor of seeing that, but mostly I went because I liked Al Sharpton. Sharpton was running for president that year, and we'd spent a fair amount of time on the road together. I'd found Sharpton amusing and insightful. Most of all, we disliked the same people, and shared loathing tends to form a bond. Since I was working at CNN at the time, hosting a show, I needed a magazine to pay for the excursion, and also to justify it. My first email was to David Remnick, editor of The New Yorker. *Al Sharpton in war zone? It seemed like a no-fail pitch. Remnick wasn't interested. His entire response: "Not my cuppa." That was it. Fun guy. Mark Warren, my editor at* Esquire, *had the opposite reaction: "Just send us the bill." I don't remember Warren asking a single question, much less mentioning politics. He loved the idea instantly. It's hard to imagine that happening now. A white conservative covering a group of black nationalists in Africa? No editor in New York would pay for that story now. It was a different time then, and I'm glad it was. Following Al Sharpton around as he pretended to be a diplomat turned out to be the most fun I ever had writing a magazine piece.*

"THE LEAGUE OF EXTRAORDINARY GENTLEMEN"

Esquire, November 2003

Five minutes before we boarded the plane to Africa, Al Sharpton called the group into a circle to pray. It struck me as a fine idea. Sharpton's plan to lead a delegation of American civil rights activists into the middle of the Liberian civil war clearly was going to require some divine support. And that was assuming we even got there. A man in the departure lounge at JFK had just finished telling me a long and disturbing story about Ghana Airways, the carrier we had chosen for the eleven-hour flight over. Apparently, much of its fleet was in Italy at the moment, impounded for debt. The rest was aging, creaky, and, given the virtually bankrupt condition of the company, spottily maintained. "Ghana Airways probably won't even exist a month from now," the man said. I was all for praying.

Fourteen of us gathered across from the gate one afternoon in late July and held hands. On my left was Sanford Rubenstein, Abner Louima's lawyer in the New York Police Department brutality case. On my right was His Eminence Franzo W. King, D.D., archbishop and lead sax player of the St. John Coltrane African Orthodox Church in San Francisco. Across the circle was former D.C. mayor Marion Barry's wife, Cora Masters Barry, and three guys from the Nation of Islam, two of them named James Muhammad. Cornel West, the writer and scholar, led the prayer. "Lord, keep us safe," West intoned as we bowed our heads. "But more important, keep us soulful."

No one looked more soulful than West himself, who was dressed, as always, like a slightly flashy undertaker: white shirt, black three-piece suit, silver pocket watch and chain. He could have been on his way to meet the next of kin. In fact, he was coming from a jazz club. West had stayed in the city until 4:00 a.m. before returning to his "crib in Jersey" (Princeton, New Jersey, where he teaches), then catching a ride to the airport. Along the way, he'd neglected to pack. West boarded the flight for Ghana with two books and a tiny carry-on the size of a woman's cosmetic case. That was it. He had no suitcases or garment bags or luggage of any kind. Nor did he have any real idea where we were going or how long we might be there. "When are we coming back?" he asked me as we walked down the ramp onto the plane.

It was not an idle question. By the morning we left, Sharpton's office had released only three days of what was supposed to be a weeklong itinerary. From what I could tell, the plan was to fly to Ghana and charter a plane from there to Liberia, where Sharpton would meet with indicted-war-criminal president Charles Taylor and talk peace. Of course, Sharpton doesn't have the standing to negotiate anything on behalf of anybody other than himself. But to get hung up on this fact is to miss the improvisational brilliance of this trip. And besides, Sharpton had actually spoken to Colin Powell about it just two days before. The State Department had raised no objection.

Once Sharpton had completed whatever it was he planned to do with Charles Taylor, we were going to leave Liberia, presumably again by charter, and head back to Ghana. Unless plans changed and we decided to fly down to South Africa for an audience with Nelson Mandela. Or something like that. At the end, we'd come home.

Those were all the details I got, and they were hard-earned. I'd first heard about the trip only five days before, when Rachel Noerdlinger, Sharpton's spokeswoman, sent me a two-sentence email: "Rev. is planning to head to Liberia this Sat. and if you want to go, call Minister Akbar Muhammad for travel details." She added that if I wanted my visa expedited, I should call a number in Brooklyn and "ask for Brian."

I called Brian first. He was friendly enough and seemed to know a lot about embassies. But when he declined to reveal his last name, I decided against sending him my passport. Next I called Akbar Muhammad. Muhammad is the international representative of the Nation of Islam and a longtime assistant to Louis Farrakhan. He was recruited into the Nation in 1960 by Malcolm X himself. A few years ago, when it looked as if

Farrakhan might die of prostate cancer, Muhammad was considered a likely successor. In the Nation of Islam, Akbar Muhammad is a big deal. In his spare time, he runs a travel agency in St. Louis.

Muhammad agreed to purchase my plane tickets and set up hotel and travel arrangements, all for a 2.5 percent processing fee. Rachel Noerdlinger seemed surprised when I told her about it. "You gave your credit card to Akbar Muhammad?" she said. "The entire Nation of Islam is going to be buying clothes on you. Louis Farrakhan's going to get a new house on your MasterCard." Actually, she assured me, "they'd get their ass in trouble if they did that."

Not that the possibility really bothered me. Sure, it would be a hassle if Louis Farrakhan bought a new house on my Master-Card. But what a story. The trip had the same sort of appeal: an African war zone. With Al Sharpton. Accompanied by a busload of black nationalists and Abner Louima's lawyer. It was hard to say exactly what it all added up to, apart from a pretty interesting scene. That was enough for me.

Midway across the Atlantic, the captain informed us that we'd be making an unscheduled stop in the Azores to refuel. It was the middle of the night when we landed on Santa Maria Island, a ten-mile-long rock with a gas pump. We were sitting on the runway in the dark when *I Love Lucy* came on.

Due to budget cuts, Ghana Airways does not provide headphones. This means that all in-flight entertainment must be piped through the plane's PA system. The effect is to make even the chirpiest dialogue sound like an Official Announcement. I knew Ricky was saying something to Lucy about her spending habits, but I couldn't shake the feeling he was talking about emergency exits and flotation devices.

Suddenly, a commotion broke out in business class. The Reverend Al Sampson, the pastor of Fernwood United Methodist Church in Chicago and a longtime friend of Sharpton's, had collared a flight attendant and was berating him about the choice of entertainment. "We're going to Africa," Sampson said, very agitated. "This is Ghana Airways. And you put this on? We shouldn't have to watch *I Love Lucy* in the year 2003."

The flight attendant was squatting in the aisle, doing his best to listen politely. He was obviously confused. Julianne Malveaux, the liberal commentator and PBS host, who happened to be sitting nearby, jumped in. "This is offensive," she said.

Overwhelmed, the flight attendant left to get his superior, who arrived at a half trot. The discussion continued at high volume for the rest of the episode. Sampson never explained precisely what was so disturbing about *I Love Lucy*. His main point seemed to be that it was a show "with no cultural context," which I took to mean that it had too many white people.

He was still stewing when we arrived in Ghana at five in the morning. On the bus to the hotel, someone mentioned a story that had run on Black Entertainment Television about Sharpton's trip to Africa. Apparently it was unflattering. Sampson made the connection immediately.

"Who owns *I Love Lucy*?" he said. "Viacom. And what's part of Viacom? BET. BET is part of Viacom."

"That's right," said someone from the back of the bus.

Sampson nodded sagely. "So you know that the disinformation is just beginning."

It was a tantalizing introduction, and I wanted to hear more. Unfortunately, before Sampson could flesh out the BET–Viacom–Ricky Ricardo nexus, we had arrived at the hotel. After a shower and a change of clothes, we were off again.

As a rule, the civil rights establishment is not punctual. But even by the standards of the chronically late, Sharpton is chronically late. Like all politicians, he tends to schedule an impossible number of events in a single day. But that's only part of the problem. Habit accounts for the rest. After spending so many years on the road, with so little cash, so far from the edge of respectability, Sharpton has lost the ability to travel like a legitimate person. In Sharpton's world, itineraries are merely suggestions. It's a measure of his awesome natural talent that he's able to get anything done at all. He's that disorganized.

One of the few commitments that Sharpton never misses is church on Sunday. He attends a service no matter where he happens to be. If you know Sharpton primarily through his political activism—or his history as a Tawana Brawley adviser or FBI informant or James Brown protégé—it can be hard to believe that he's actually a Christian clergyman. Doubts disappear when you hear him preach.

Sharpton preaches like a man who has been doing it since before he could read or write. (He was only four when he gave his first sermon on John 14 in front of nine hundred people at the Washington Temple Church of God in Christ in Brooklyn.) His sermons are as extemporaneous as his schedule. Not a word is written down; everything is subject to change. Often he switches the topic of a sermon midway through in response to what he feels from the crowd. Sometimes he bursts into song.

Most surprising of all, there's a fair amount of religion in Sharpton's preaching. He quotes at length from the Bible, talks without embarrassment about Jesus and redemption and heaven and hell. He believes in the supernatural and says so. He's probably the only Democratic presidential candidate this year who is comfortable discussing faith healing, prophesies, and speaking in tongues, all of which he has seen and is convinced are real.

Sharpton was scheduled to preach at Calvary Baptist Church in downtown Accra the first morning of the trip. We arrived more than an hour late. Annoyed, the pastor interrupted Sharpton's sermon after just five minutes. For the rest of the service, the congregation sang. Archbishop King of the Church of Coltrane stood in front of the altar in full clerical regalia, playing the saxophone. Two local men played the congas. Women danced in the aisles. Cornel West hugged me for the second time that morning. After a few minutes, Sharpton got a call on his satellite phone and went outside.

It was Jewel Taylor, the first lady of Liberia, calling from Monrovia once again to offer the spare bedroom in the presidential palace for our scheduled visit the next day. Sharpton was polite but skeptical. "We'll call her tomorrow morning," he said once he got off the phone. "If she doesn't answer, we'll know what that means."

At some point during our flight across the Atlantic, Charles

Taylor had lost control of his country. Two rebel armies—Liberians United for Reconciliation and Democracy, known as LURD; and the Movement for Democracy in Liberia, known as MODEL—appeared to have taken everything but downtown Monrovia. LURD was said to be within ten miles of Taylor's home.

Liberia has been in a state of low-grade revolution since at least 1980, when a twenty-eight-year-old master sergeant named Samuel Doe executed virtually the entire leadership of the country, most of them descendants of freed American slaves. President Doe himself met his end ten years later, when he had the misfortune of being captured by a guerrilla leader known as General Prince Johnson. Johnson force-fed Doe his own penis, then cut off his ears and rolled him around Monrovia in a wheelbarrow until he died, videotaping the whole thing for posterity. The country went downhill from there. Taylor knew he had little hope for mercy if LURD made it to his house.

Which, it occurred to me, might explain why he seemed so eager to have Sharpton come visit. When you're facing slow death by acetylene torch, even a third-tier American presidential candidate can look like a lifeline. If Taylor did have to meet his enemies face-to-face, Sharpton might help him talk his way out of being castrated. In Africa as in Brooklyn, Sharpton is famous for being a good talker.

A similar thought had occurred to LURD, as I discovered when I called CNN's producer in Liberia. The network had asked me to bring a box of audio equipment to the CNN crew in Monrovia, which had essentially been stranded in the city when

2f

THE LONG SLIDE

commercial air service was suspended the week before. The producer wasn't bullish on Sharpton's prospects of success. LURD was well aware he was coming, he said. They viewed the trip as an effort to prop up Taylor. LURD might try to kill Sharpton at the airport, the producer explained, or possibly at one of the roadblocks on the long drive into the city. It "would be brave" to come to Liberia tomorrow, he said.

The producer said one other thing. Actually, he didn't come right out and say it, because foreign correspondents, particularly Australian ones, almost never admit they're afraid, even when they're bleeding or on fire or falling out of airplanes. But the tone of his voice indicated that Monrovia was getting unruly. He and the other foreign press were hunkered in the U.S. embassy compound. Outside, Taylor's troops were fighting street battles with LURD forces. Many of the soldiers on both sides were barely in their teens. Some of the LURD forces were dressed in women's clothes—wedding dresses, blond wigs, high heels—and were deranged from huffing gasoline. It sounded like an uncomfortable scene.

If Sharpton was aware of what was happening in Liberia, he didn't show it. He just nodded when Akbar Muhammad explained that we'd be taking an ambulance plane into Monrovia after breakfast. He didn't flinch when told that LURD had just seized the airport. None of it seemed to bother him.

An hour later we drove to a hotel in Accra, where representatives of LURD, MODEL, and the Taylor government were holding "peace talks." The talks had been going on for six weeks, during which time, all sides agreed, nothing had been accomplished. Sharpton had decided it would be a good venue for his diplomatic skills.

Late in the afternoon, about thirty Liberian factional representatives and exile leaders filed into a room off the lobby of the M Plaza Hotel. Sharpton was sitting at the head table, alongside Archbishop King, Rev. Sampson, Cornel West, and Marjorie Harris, the capable, good-natured director of Sharpton's National Action Network. The idea was for Sharpton to moderate a discussion among all sides, as a disinterested third party. I believe that was the idea.

The secretary general of the National Patriotic Party, Taylor's man in Accra, spoke first. "The U.S. has been the drum major behind problems in Liberia," he began. With that in mind, the United States government should take steps to atone for its sins, mostly by not helping anybody who might be seeking to replace Charles Taylor. That, said the secretary general, would be "rewarding rebellion."

A representative from an anti-Taylor group immediately objected. His name was Mohammed Kromah, and he identified himself as the head of something called the Union of Liberian Associations in the Americas. When not conducting diplomacy in West Africa, Kromah is a supervisor at the Maryland Department of Human Resources in Baltimore. Kromah, like most Liberians outside the Taylor government, had seen relatives and friends die in the endless cycle of wars and was desperate for U.S. intervention. He spoke passionately about the historic ties between the United States and Liberia. He pleaded for American troops to come and end the killing. Finally, Al Sampson cut him off.

Sampson, a heavyset man in his sixties who is partial to gold chains and safari suits, began by describing himself as "the man who was ordained by Martin King." Then he launched into what was perhaps the most patronizing lecture that I have ever personally witnessed. Addressing Kromah, Sampson explained that the very idea of sending U.S. troops to Liberia was immoral. African-American soldiers fighting in Africa? That would be "black-on-black violence." Indeed, it would constitute a kind of civil war within the African diaspora. "The problem is," Sampson thundered, "we ain't seeing each other as brothers."

That was for sure. Apart from skin tone, Sampson has more in common with Trent Lott than with the people he was haranguing. The average Liberian, it turns out, does not share the same assumptions as the average black Methodist minister from Chicago. "He doesn't understand," Mohammed Kromah said to me later. "Being brothers because we're all black. It sounds good. But when there were riots in Los Angeles after Rodney King, did they ask gang leaders to get together and talk? No, they took them to court. They sent police."

It was a good point, but Kromah had to wait a long time to make it. The Reverend Sampson was just getting started. By the time he got to our upcoming trip to the war zone, he had a faraway look in his eyes.

"Nobody in the White House is prepared to step into Liberia tomorrow to live or die," Sampson said. But we are. Because we cannot know the hour that God will call us home. We cannot know when our work on this earth is done. We can only do our duty. As Martin did. As Malcolm did. As Ron Brown did.

For, like them, we have been to the mountaintop. And we are unafraid.

Or something like that. My notes trail off after the first die. I was too mesmerized to keep writing. Sampson seemed delighted by the idea of buying it in Liberia. You could tell he was imagining the headlines back home: "Spiritual Leader Slain on Quest for Peace: Chicagoland Minister Leaves Legacy of Healing."

I wasn't on board. For one thing, I hadn't been to the mountaintop yet. For another, my kids would miss me if I got killed. And since when did Ron Brown, Clinton's commerce secretary, get inducted into the pantheon of civil rights martyrs?

By dinner, details of the chaos in Liberia were all over CNN, but as far as I know, no one in the group piped up to suggest that flying in might be a bad idea. I didn't. Around midnight I headed back to my room, feeling slightly ill. As I passed through the lobby, I saw Archbishop King sitting alone against a wall. I liked King. It's easy to mock a man who has founded a religion based on John Coltrane, who considers *A Love Supreme,* whatever its merits as a jazz album, to be holy scripture. It's hard to take a man like that too seriously, and I confess that my first instinct was not to. But after spending a week with him, I can report that His Eminence Franzo W. King is a genuinely spiritual man.

He certainly talks like one. King tends to speak in riddles and dictums and parables, and at an almost inaudible volume. One day I told him that I considered some person or other a bit of a phony. King looked at me intently for a moment, then put his hand on the back of my head and pulled my ear to his lips. "Is a tree phony because it loses its leaves in winter?" he whispered.

I suspect that Archbishop King did a ton of acid at some point. Either that or he really is a mystic. I'm still not sure, and that night I didn't care. I wanted to know what he thought of our impending trip to Monrovia. He didn't answer the question directly, of course. Instead he quoted John Coltrane: "During Vietnam, they asked Coltrane what he thought of the war. He said, 'I'm against all wars.'" King looked at me and nodded slowly. I nodded back, then said good night and went to bed.

In the end, the question of whether or not to go to Monrovia was settled by the pilot of the ambulance plane. The next morning he refused to fly in, on the grounds that we'd get killed. Apparently he hadn't been to the mountaintop yet, either.

Sharpton accepted the news like the flexible traveler he is and immediately began planning peace talks of his own at our hotel. The logistics weren't complicated, since much of the leadership of LURD happened to be staying on the same floor. They were all over the hotel at all hours and very hard to miss. They were the sinister ones with guns. I didn't meet anyone affiliated with LURD who didn't look as if he'd just returned from a long but enjoyable day of summary executions.

One morning I was sitting in the lobby interviewing Ruth Perry, who for a brief time during the 1990s was the president of Liberia and lived to tell about it. With her was a fellow Liberian named Marie Parker. Parker was also unusually lucky, having made the last charter flight out of Monrovia the day before.

While her plane taxied down the runway, LURD troops lobbed mortars onto the tarmac. Looking out the window, she saw a child decapitated by shrapnel.

As Mrs. Parker told her story and Mrs. Perry gasped, a tall man dressed entirely in black approached the table, pulled up a chair, and sat down. He did not remove his sunglasses. He introduced himself as Lieutenant General Donzo of LURD. The outline of a handgun stood out in relief against his leg. He smiled at the women. They glared back.

Unprompted, Donzo gave the three of us an update on the fighting in Monrovia. "Mr. Taylor cannot escape," he said. "We will catch him. Mr. Taylor is on a suicide mission now. We could run the whole city in seventy-two hours."

Donzo grinned and fiddled with his cell phone, which he said he used to command his fourteen-year-old transvestite gas-sniffing troops in the field. It was a newish Nokia, with internet service and a built-in camera. Aiming it across the room, he took a picture of an air-conditioning unit to show off the picture quality. Donzo claimed to be thirty-five, but I'd bet my car he was at least ten years younger.

I remembered a piece of propaganda I had seen, produced by the Taylor government, that accused LURD soldiers of practicing cannibalism and human sacrifice. I was glad when Lieutenant General Donzo left the table.

Sharpton wanted every member of the delegation at the first round of his peace talks, scheduled for 9:00 p.m. in a conference room at the hotel. LURD agreed to come, though it wasn't clear whether its members understood what they were coming to.

(LURD's deputy secretary general told me that he was looking forward to talking to "Ashcroft" at the meeting.) Cornel West had high hopes nonetheless. "This is going to set the tone for the post-cold-war era," he said with real enthusiasm.

The LURD guys were precisely on time. They walked in as a group with their heads down, like tenth graders late for class, and sat together in the third row. Representatives from Taylor's government were supposed to come, too, but at the last minute they didn't show, claiming they were caught in traffic.

Undaunted, Sharpton reached Sam Jackson, Taylor's unusually slick minister of economic affairs, on his cell phone. Sharpton carried on the conversation while the rest of the room listened. "These brothers have come to the table," he said, referring to the LURD guys, who were still sitting with their heads down. "They're willing to talk. You've got to respond." Jackson said he'd call back with an offer.

Cornel West, meanwhile, had started a one-man teach-in, a complex rap on the struggle for indigenous self-determination in the postcolonial era. It sounded a lot like a graduate seminar on third-world politics. "The alternative to bloodshed is dialogue," West said. "The dialogue has to be one where reasons have weight. The Liberian people will have to take their future in their own hands. What we all want to avoid is some sort of imperial imposition."

Before it was over, I'm fairly sure West had used the term "dialectic" several times, possibly even "paradigm." The LURD guys obviously didn't understand a word of it. They sat in perfect silence for the duration. At one point, a cell phone went off in the LURD row, ringing the theme from Woody Woodpecker. No one answered it.

Sam Jackson called back at 9:40 with Taylor's latest offer, which sounded suspiciously like the offer he'd been making all along: if the United States was willing to send peacekeepers to Monrovia, Taylor would leave the country within a day and allow an interim government, with representatives from both rebel factions, to take his place.

Sharpton sounded skeptical: "If Taylor equivocates, I will blast him all over the world as a liar." Jackson offered his strongest reassurances. All right, said Sharpton, "I'll get Cornel and them to draft a statement." The deal was almost done.

All that remained was to convince the LURD delegation. In theory, it should have been easy. The points Taylor had agreed to—U.S. troops, exile in Nigeria, an interim government—were precisely those that LURD said it was fighting for. The problem wasn't with details. It was with comprehension. The LURD guys were utterly confused.

Sharpton tried his best. He explained the deal at least three times, each time with increasing vehemence. By the end, he was preaching, every sentence ending with the rhetorical "Is that right?" Unfortunately, the typical African warlord doesn't know much about the customs of the American black church. Sharpton's call-and-response routine left them even more bewildered.

Finally, the leader of the LURD delegation stopped Sharpton to ask a question. (He may have even raised his hand.) Does the deal include a cease-fire? Do we have to stop fighting? he wanted to know.

Sharpton looked as if he were going to drop dead of exasperation. "Of course there's got to be a cease-fire!" You morons.

I imagine it had been a long time since anyone had spoken that way to LURD leaders and lived to tell about it. The meeting broke up shortly after. Sharpton dismissed the LURD contingent like a class. "We'll be back to you in a few hours," he said. "We got your numbers." They shuffled out obediently.

There were several more meetings over the next few days. For a short time it looked as though Sharpton might have achieved a breakthrough. LURD seemed to figure out most of what was going on. Taylor appeared to be getting more flexible. On the third day, the State Department sent a foreign service officer from the Africa desk in Washington to brief Sharpton on Liberian politics. (Sharpton had spoken again to Colin Powell.) I ran into him at lunch. "I don't have a position on the Sharpton Plan, official or unofficial," he said.

Then it all fell apart. Predictably, the plan unraveled when it reached the LURD troops. They didn't want to stop fighting. When called by their commanders from the hotel coffee shop in Ghana and told about the cease-fire, the pantyhose-clad guerrillas in Monrovia simply hung up the phone. As any parent knows, fourteen-year-olds can be hard to control.

Suddenly, the bring-peace-to-Liberia portion of the trip was over. There was talk of heading to Johannesburg to see Nelson Mandela, but no one could find his number. We spent the next few days sightseeing, visiting a refugee camp, and following Sharpton as he made campaignlike stops around Accra, including a remarkably contentious interview on *Good Evening, Ghana*. The rest of the time, we sat around talking about religion, death, and politics.

The Nation of Islam guys turned out to be terrific conversationalists, the two James Muhammads in particular. They were sharp and informed and extremely polite. The most striking thing about them, though, was how relentlessly normal they seemed. Both had been loyal members of the Nation of Islam for more than twenty years. Presumably they believed, as NOI doctrine teaches, that the white race is intrinsically evil and will be incinerated by an enormous spaceship currently hovering above the earth. You'd never guess it from talking to them.

The first James Muhammad, James G., was at the time the editor of the *Final Call,* NOI's weekly newspaper and a forum for every conceivable crackpot racialist view. In his heart, James G. may be convinced that Jewish doctors are injecting black babies with AIDS, but he could not have been nicer to me. Almost every morning he called or came by my room to make sure I was awake. Once we got home, he sent me digital pictures of the trip. He ended his email with a smiley face.

The second James Muhammad, James L. (formerly James 10X), was if anything even gentler and more friendly. An accountant in the dean's office at Yale, he confided to me that his first love was photojournalism. "If I could come back as anything, I'd be a *National Geographic* photographer," he said.

I decided that it was their sincere belief in black supremacy that made the James Muhammads such good company. From their point of view, I was an irredeemable White Devil, cursed by Allah and marked for destruction. They had nothing to prove to me; I was like the retarded kid. We got along great. At the end of the trip, James L. pronounced me an honorary member of the Nation of Islam: Tucker X.

Only occasionally were there reminders that the Nation of Islam is not a mainstream religious organization. One afternoon, I called the CNN news desk and learned that Uday and Qusay Hussein had been killed by American troops in Iraq. At dinner I mentioned the news to Akbar Muhammad. He looked crestfallen. "That's unfortunate," he said. Akbar had known the Hussein boys, as well as their father. He reminisced about their time together in prewar Baghdad.

As the NOI's chief diplomat, Akbar seemed to spend most of his time traveling to the world's most repressive dictatorships. I forgot to ask him if he'd made it to North Korea, but he'd been just about everywhere else. Occasionally he'd drop references to "Brother Qaddafi" or the meal he had recently shared with Robert Mugabe, the lunatic of Zimbabwe.

On our final day in Ghana, Akbar mentioned another old friend, Idi Amin. Amin had slipped into a coma that week at a hospital in Jedda, Saudi Arabia, and wasn't expected to recover. This put Akbar in a sentimental mood. He told me about the first time he met Idi. It was 1977. The two had strolled through downtown Kampala, which at the time was "safe and quiet." If Amin dies, Akbar said, and CNN decides to run an obituary, "maybe you can present the other side."

Sharpton laughed when I told him about the conversation.

He seemed amused by the Nation of Islam, whose theology he summarized as "no booze, pork, or white women." Sharpton is widely regarded by white people as a racist, and it is true that he used to make references to "crackers" in his speeches. ("I ain't never worked for a cracker in my life," he once boasted.) He doesn't talk like that anymore. Sharpton still rails against the White Power Structure, but these days he reserves his harshest rhetoric for black people.

During a speech at the W. E. B. Du Bois center in Accra, Sharpton came off as something approaching conservative. He described black gang members as "savages" engaged in "crass, despicable, irresponsible behavior." He all but denounced hip-hop culture and the "irrelevant Negroes" it produces. "DuBois didn't come here to teach Ghanaians how to break-dance or call their grandmother 'bitch,'" Sharpton said. Decency, hard work, academic excellence—that, said Sharpton, is the path to dignity and self-improvement.

Al Sampson, meanwhile, continued to do a spot-on impression of the early Malcolm X. I made it to breakfast one morning just in time to catch him in mid-rant. If you're looking for a single cause of all the world's problems, Sampson was saying, look no further than the white race. He glanced up and saw me, the physical embodiment of eons of injustice and oppression. "When are you going to stop trashing the universe?" he said.

I should have laughed it off, but it was just too early. What a vicious, ignorant thing to say, I replied.

Ignorant? he said. Are you saying I have a low IQ?

Before I could answer, Sampson began to tick off a list of

white crimes against humanity, beginning with the slave trade. As it happened, Sharpton was planning to visit a slavery museum that very day. I'll be watching you when we get there, Sampson said. "I want to see if you even cry."

I was close to the snapping point. After days of needling from Sampson, I was being poisoned by a toxic buildup of dislike. I longed for the cathartic release that would come from leaping across the table and smashing his nose. I must have telegraphed it, because both James Muhammads immediately tried to calm me down. "Come on back, now," said James L. "Come on back." Archbishop King didn't say anything, but walked over and gave me a hug.

Sampson was trying to make me feel guilty. It wasn't obvious to me at the time. The idea that I'd be responsible for the sins (or, for that matter, share in the glory of the accomplishments) of dead people who happened to share my skin tone has always confused me. Racial solidarity wasn't a working concept in my Southern California hometown. Most people barely had last names, much less ethnic identities. I grew up feeling about as much connection to nineteenth-century slave owners as I did to bus drivers in Helsinki or astronomers in Tirana. We're all capable of getting sunburned. That's it.

I tried a couple of times to explain this to Rev. Sampson. But "your people," he'd say, did this or that appalling thing. I don't have any "people," I'd reply. Beyond my immediate family, I don't speak for anybody. The deceased bad guys you're talking about, we just look alike.

Either he didn't get it, or he didn't believe me. Day after day,

Sampson kept it up, trying his best to make me feel bad about myself for being a universe trasher. I never did. Ultimately, I'm just not a guilty white person.

Maybe that's why Sharpton and I got along so well. We talked for hours over the course of the week, about everything from marriage to the Iowa caucuses. By the end, I'd settled at least one question: Sharpton doesn't hate whites after all. He just hates white liberals.

"You've dealt with inoffensive Negroes," Sharpton roared, imagining that he was talking to Terry McAuliffe or some other Democratic Party official. "Now you've got to deal with Al Sharpton." Sharpton knows that many white Democrats are embarrassed that he exists. The street-hustler wardrobe, Tawana Brawley, the hair—he is a public-relations disaster for the Democratic Party, a living explanation of why suburbanites vote Republican. The thought fills him with pleasure, because it means that he has the power to make white Democrats uncomfortable every time he speaks.

Which is why he can hardly wait for the Democratic National Convention next summer in Boston. "Let me put it this way: I can speak inside or outside. They can choose the venue. But either way, I'm speaking in prime time." Either speech, he points out, will almost certainly be carried live on the networks.

"The only people who don't respect me are white liberals," he said one night at dinner. Some have dismissed him outright as a buffoon (he became furious just thinking about it); others have merely patted him on the head and tried to send him on his way. That's how it felt, anyway. He saw it happen to Jesse

Jackson, who started out as an independent man of the left and wound up a party hack, summoned to the Clinton White House periodically like a servant to perform.

They got Jackson little by little, Sharpton believes, mostly by giving him things: money, jobs for his friends, the use of private airplanes. Within a year or two, Jackson was an employee. Sharpton considers it a profound political lesson. "I saw what happened to Jesse. I was there. They're assuming I want what Jesse wanted."

If so, they're wrong. Sharpton has never taken federal grants. He doesn't want patronage. He's happy to fly commercial. "What can they give me? A couple hundred grand in voter-registration money? Please. I don't need that. I don't need anything from them. They can't control me. That's why they hate me."

What does Al Sharpton want? He didn't even pause when I asked. "What we want is them." By them Sharpton means every white liberal in the leadership of the Democratic Party who has ever assumed a high-handed tone with him, put him off for a meeting, or in any way acted supercilious or superior in his presence. That's a lot of people. Sharpton says he'll start by demanding control over the chairmanship of the party. From there, he'd like a hand in picking next year's vice presidential nominee. After that, we'll see.

Sharpton understands he may not get everything he wants. They might continue to patronize him. That's fine, too. He could always pull a Nader and go third party. "That's up to them," he said between bites of chicken. "If I buy a suit and the pants split, I need to get it fixed or get a new suit. My butt is out. My behind is getting cold in the wind." The question you have to ask at that point, he said, is: "Do I need to get a new suit? Or do you have a needle and thread?"

Sharpton has thought all of this through in some detail. He's fairly certain Democratic leaders consider him incapable of formulating a serious strategy. "I've got a plan. They never thought of that. They're used to—at best—a shakedown."

And that's only Sharpton's plan for the next year. He said he intends to come up with new demands by 2006, when Senator Hillary Clinton comes up for reelection. New York is one place Sharpton has uncontested influence. He could cause Senator Clinton a significant headache if he ran against her in the primary or withheld his endorsement in the general election. Like his convention speech, that thought pleases him.

None of this has escaped Bill Clinton's notice. Clinton called Sharpton in July to set up a meeting. Sharpton assumes the former president wanted to get a sense of what the demands might be. When the meeting takes place, Sharpton said, "I won't give up anything. It's not to my advantage for him to figure me out."

In the end, of course, Sharpton isn't really running for president of the United States. He's running for president of black America. In some ways, with the rest of the traditional civil rights leadership aging or retired, he has already won.

We left for the slavery museum later that morning. It was about a hundred miles up the coast by bus. Akbar Muhammad sat in the front with a microphone, acting as our tour guide. As we rolled through an outdoor market, he ruminated on the tragedy of the modern African diet. Until colonization, he explained, Africans did not eat pork. "It was the white man who brought the pig."

The travelogue/history lesson went on for about an hour. Finally Akbar paused. He rooted around in his bag and produced a cassette. "I hope you don't mind," he said, popping it into the dash. "This is one of my favorite tapes."

I don't know what I expected. A speech by Minister Farrakhan, maybe, or the Protocols of the Elders of Zion, as read by Amiri Baraka. And then it started. Strumming my pain with his fingers. Akbar cranked it up. Sharpton picked up the tune. Singing my life with his words. Cornel West started to dance in his seat. Killing me softly with his song, killing me softly. With his song. The whole bus was singing with Roberta Flack now, the James Muhammads taking the lead. Akbar rewound the song and played it again. After that we listened to Lou Rawls.

The slavery museum was at Cape Coast Castle, a massive former British customs house, which for more than a hundred years was used as a holding pen for slaves bound for the Americas. Single file and in silence, we walked down stone steps into the slave dungeon. Inside, it was as dark as a cave but hotter, with a single barred window fifteen feet up the wall. Akbar explained that the shallow channel carved into the floor had been the slaves' only latrine. He asked us to observe a moment of silence in their memory. We stood in a circle holding hands with our heads down. Someone began to sing a Negro spiritual, a cappella. Then the sobbing started.

It began, I think, with Cornel West. Soon it had spread

to Sharpton and Akbar, and even to the notably white Sandy Rubenstein, who told me later that he was overcome by the thought of his own forebears enslaved by Pharaoh. Within a minute, the stone walls echoed with the sounds of a dozen people weeping, wailing, and gasping for breath. Al Sampson sounded as if he was about to die.

I felt like a voyeur. I closed my eyes while crying men shouted out the names of deceased ancestors. Someone passed out candles, and the group sang "We Shall Overcome." Sharpton, Cornel West, Sampson, and Akbar closed the ceremony with prayers. West thanked God for Sharpton, whom he described as a leader "in the tradition of John Coltrane, Curtis Mayfield, and Gladys Knight." I was sweating profusely.

Cornel West, I noticed, was not. I looked at him closely as he prayed. Though it was at least 100 degrees in the dungeon, he had not taken off his coat or loosened his tie. (I never once saw him do either.) He had on the same clothes he'd been wearing when we boarded the plane in New York six days before. They looked perfect. There was not a speck of lint or dandruff or dust on his suit. His shoes were shined, the creases in his trousers crisp. His shirt was so white it looked luminescent. The next day I broke down and asked him how, with no change of clothes, he managed to stay so clean. He laughed cryptically but didn't answer. I began to suspect that I was witnessing some sort of supernatural event, a low-grade miracle. I still can't think of a better explanation.

Finally we emerged from the dungeon and stood around squinting in the sunlight. Al Sampson walked over to where I was standing. His face was puffy from crying. He put his hands on my shoulders. For a moment I was certain he was going to bite me. Instead, he looked into my eyes and smiled. "I love you, man," he said.

From that moment until we parted at the baggage claim at JFK, Sampson treated me like an old friend.

We left Ghana the next day, or tried to. True to its reputation, Ghana Airways was thirteen hours late leaving Accra. No sooner had we reached altitude than the pilot announced we'd be making an unscheduled stop in Banjul, Gambia, for more fuel. On the ground in Gambia, Marjorie Harris, Sharpton's closest aide, called New York from her satellite phone to check in. There were a lot of messages. The most pressing was from the family of James Davis, a New York City councilman who had been shot to death the day before at City Hall. Davis's family wanted Sharpton's support—not just his moral support, but money to pay for the funeral, as well as related "expenses." Harris opposed the idea. The office was already in debt. Not two months before, one of Sharpton's cars had been repossessed for late payments.

Sharpton said he had no choice but to send the Davis family money. "I can't believe he didn't have insurance, but I guess he didn't." Harris appeared to be completely unconvinced. "We've got to help," Sharpton said. And so he agreed to. He looked tired, but also resigned. The president, he knows, is never off duty.

_____

This is the only architecture piece I've ever written, but it's a subject I think about all the time. You learn a lot about a society from its buildings. Are they beautiful? Do they serve the people who live in them? Do they last? You could ask the same questions of a civilization. By those measures, the British Empire fares well. The English, whatever you think of them, planted pretty buildings around the world. It may be the most unusual thing they ever did. Certainly no one's done it since. I wrote this story on the flight home from Bombay. Twelve hours later, I landed in Washington, a city that hasn't constructed a graceful public building in fifty years. It made me wonder about our own empire.

"TUCKER CARLSON'S DIARY: THE AESTHETIC MERITS OF BRITISH COLONIALISM"

Spectator, March 3, 2016

J ust as the presidential race in America started to get really crazy, I left for India. On the morning of the South Carolina primary, I interviewed Donald Trump from a restaurant near the state capitol. By the next afternoon I was dodging mopeds in a traffic circle in Mumbai. I'd imagined the trip as a respite from the campaign, much needed after weeks of immersion in a world where Bernie Sanders is considered charming and Hillary Clinton is regarded as an intellectual. Yet I found that I couldn't stop thinking about the race. If you're brooding about the future of your country, a former British colony is the wrong place to do it. It suggests too much.

The first thing you notice about Mumbai is the first thing

you notice about every place the British once occupied, which is how much of themselves they left there. The United States spent over a decade and trillions of dollars in Iraq, and the only physical evidence that remains is a concrete embassy compound, some airstrips, and a sea of steel shipping containers. Maybe because they never considered that they might leave, the British built entire cities out of stone, with railways to connect them. And they did it with reliably good taste. Too often lost in the hand-wringing over the evils of colonialism is the aesthetic contribution of the British Empire. The Brits tended to colonize beautiful places and make them prettier. Bermuda, New Zealand, Fiji, Cape Town—notice a theme? Style wasn't an ancillary benefit; it was part of the point. Behind every Gurkha regiment marched a battalion of interior designers.

English taste seemed to improve with distance. At home, nineteenth-century British architecture tended toward excess, layers of rococo baubles alternating with blocky overkill. Abroad, the form became more flexible, often incorporating local features like Moorish arches and minarets. (Contrast this with the French, to whom every colony was a chance to re-create an outer ring of Paris.) The average English customs house on a minor Bahamian island enhances its surroundings more than anything Frank Lloyd Wright ever built. More durable, too. British colonial buildings were the most appealing structures in virtually every city the empire controlled. Fifty years later, they often still are. When he seized power in Pakistan, Pervez Musharraf never even pretended to settle in the new PM's residence in Islamabad. He headed for the old British headquarters in Rawalpindi, where he sat beneath ceiling fans sipping Scotch and reading Flashman novels.

Nowhere is the architectural contrast starker and more jarring than in Mumbai. India is on its way to becoming a rich country, and Mumbai is its financial capital. Signs of wealth abound, from ubiquitous cranes to the mobile phones that every chai vendor carries. Fewer people seem to be living on the streets of downtown Mumbai than in midtown Manhattan. The good news is there's a building boom under way. The bad news is, the results are appalling. Much of the new architecture is ugly, of course, straight from the Soviet-occupied-Poland school of design, but the construction is also shoddy. Buildings put up ten years ago are streaked with rust from exposed rebar, their concrete peeling apart in flakes. Even the newest blocks seem temporary or half-finished, as if nobody cared enough to complete the job. Not unlike post-invasion Baghdad, actually.

Meanwhile, at the south end of town, the Raj still dominates the skyline, and breathtakingly so. Is there a more attractive clock building outside Europe than the Rajabai Tower, completed in 1878? Does America have a single railway station that compares to the one Mumbai commuters have used since 1887? A single post office more impressive than the one the British built there in 1913? A more majestic municipal building than the Bombay High Court? The old section of Mumbai amounts to an open-air time capsule, substantially unchanged from the day Dickie and Edwina Mountbatten flew back to London. Unfortunately, nobody has cleaned up since. The old buildings are filthy and neglected, with broken shutters, missing windows, and front lawns piled with rubbish. Just a block or two from the Taj Mahal Hotel, near the ocean in one of the priciest parts of the city, there's a row of wooden Victorian houses, large and ornate and beautiful. It looks like a postcard, but walk closer. The roofs have been patched with blue nylon tarps. The porches sag where the support beams have rotted. Each one verges on collapse.

There's something crushingly sad about all this, but also instructive. Empires end, usually more quickly than expected. They're not always replaced by something better. Worth remembering at election time.

―――――――

You don't hear his name much anymore, but for a time Congressman Ron Paul, M.D., of Galveston was an ideological force in American politics. His son, Rand, is now a U.S. senator from Kentucky. Paul was certainly the purest libertarian ever to run for president. He believed in your absolute right to do whatever you wanted, as long as it didn't infringe on his rights, and he sincerely meant it. Millions of people loved him for this. Many others, especially in Washington, hated him for it. At the end of 2007, I was fired from my job hosting a not-very-successful show on MSNBC. With some unexpected time on my hands, I decided to meet up with Ron Paul on the road to assess the phenomenon. I happened to be present for Paul's first-ever encounter with prostitution.

"PIMP MY RIDE"

The New Republic, December 31, 2007

The first thing I learned from driving around Nevada with Ron Paul for a couple of days: people really hate the Federal Reserve. This became clear midway through a speech Paul was giving to a group of Republicans at a community center in Pahrump, a dusty town about sixty miles west of Las Vegas. Pahrump is known for its legal brothels (Heidi Fleiss lives there), but most of the people in the audience looked more like ranchers than swingers. They stood five deep at the back of the room and listened politely as the candidate spoke.

Until Paul got to the part about the Fed. "We need a much better monetary system," he said, a system based on "sound money, money that's backed by something." Paul, who is small and delicate and has a high voice, spoke in a near monotone, making no effort to excite the audience. They cheered anyway.

Then he said this: "The Constitution gives no authority for a central bank." The crowd went wild, or as wild as a group of sober Republicans can on a Monday night. They hooted and yelled and stomped their feet. Paul stopped speaking for a moment, his words drowned out. Then he continued on about monetary policy.

Wow, I thought. The constitutionality of a central bank is not an issue you see on many lists of voter concerns. (How many pollsters would think to ask about it? How many voters would understand the question?) Yet a room full of non-economists had just responded feverishly when Paul brought it up. Hoping for some context, I went outside and found a Paul staffer. He didn't sound surprised when I told him about the speech. "It's our biggest applause line," he said.

One thing you can say for certain: the crowds at Ron Paul rallies aren't coming to be entertained. Stylistically, a Paul speech is about as colorful as a tax return. He is the only politician I've ever seen who doesn't draw energy from the audience; his tone is as flat at the conclusion as it was at the beginning. There are no jokes. There's no warm-up, no shout-out to local luminaries in the room, no inspiring vignettes about ordinary Americans doing their best in the face of this or that bad thing. In fact, there are virtually none of the usual political clichés in a Paul speech. Children may be our future, but Ron Paul isn't admitting it in public.

Paul is no demagogue, and probably couldn't be if he tried. He's too libertarian. He can't stand to tell other people what to do, even people who've shown up looking for instructions. On board the campaign's tiny chartered jet one night (the plane was so small my legs were intertwined with the candidate's for the entire flight), Paul and his staff engaged in an unintentionally hilarious exchange about the cabin lights. The staff wanted to know whether Paul preferred the lights on or off. Not wanting to be bossy, Paul wouldn't say. Ultimately, the staff had to guess. It was a long three minutes.

Being at the center of attention clearly bothers Paul. "I like to be unnoticed," he says, a claim not typically made by presidential candidates. "That's my personality. I see all the excitement and sometimes I say to myself, 'Why do they do that?' I don't see myself as a big deal." Ordinarily you'd have to dismiss a line like that out of hand—if he's so humble, why is he running for president?—but, in Paul's case, it might be true. In fact, it might be the key to his relative success. His fans don't read his awkwardness as a social phobia, but as a sign of authenticity. Paul never outshines his message, which is unchanging: let adults make their own choices; liberty works. For a unified theory of everything, it's pretty simple. And Paul sincerely believes it.

Most Republicans, of course, profess to believe it, too. But only Paul has introduced a bill to legalize unpasteurized milk. Give yourself five minutes and see if you can think of a more countercultural idea than that. Most people assume that the whole reason we have a government is to make sure the milk gets pasteurized. It takes some stones to argue otherwise, especially if nobody's paying you to do it. (The raw-milk lobby basically consists of about eight goat-cheese enthusiasts in Manhattan, and possibly the Amish.) Paul is pro-choice on pasteurization entirely for reasons of principle. "I support the right of people to drink whatever they want," he says. He mocks the idea that "only government can make sure we're safe, so we need the government to protect us. I don't think we'd all die of unsafe food if we didn't have the FDA. Someone else would do it." If you know Ron Paul primarily from watching the Republican debates, you probably assume he spends most of his time ranting about September 11 and the Iraq invasion. In fact, his real passion is Austrian economics. More even than the war, Paul despises paper currency, which he considers a hoax, "fiat money." He can become emotional talking about it. Caught in traffic in downtown Vegas on the way to an event, Paul looked out the window at the casinos and mused aloud: "Can you imagine when all those slot machines used real silver dollars? All that silver . . ." His words trailed off, as in a pleasant daydream.

Paul trusts coins, and he has bought them all his life, first as a childhood collector, then as an investor. During the 1980s, as he ran unsuccessfully for the Senate and the White House, he became involved in a coin business, Ron Paul Coins. Numismatics, he says, is a labor of love. "You only make five or ten dollars a coin. You've got to sell a lot of coins to get rich. I was just promoting something I believe in." It's a rare person who admits something like this. Everybody knows the gold standard is for cranks. It's complicated, unwieldy, and basically incompatible with the modern world. Worse, it's boring. Paul doesn't care. "It's been over one hundred years since that issue has been talked about in a presidential election," he told me with apparent pride.

Over dinner at the coffee shop in the Saddle West Hotel, Casino, and RV Resort, Paul and his staff talked about little else. There were eight or nine of us at the table, with the seventy-two-year-old obstetrician-congressman at the head in a gray suit, working over a chicken platter and discussing hard money. It had the feel of a familiar conversation, a dialogue that doesn't really end but that never diminishes in intensity. At one point, Paul's assistant checked his BlackBerry for the latest gold and silver prices and read them aloud to the table.

For Paul, the original sin in monetary policy took place in 1933, when FDR uncoupled the currency from gold. This removed limits from federal spending, allowing Congress an endless supply of money it could print at will, while leaving citizens vulnerable to the inflation that inevitably resulted. But, worst of all from Paul's point of view, it was compulsory. Private currencies are forbidden, so Americans had no choice but to participate. The whole system is a mandatory Ponzi scheme, built on faith in the government. Except that, now that the bottom has dropped out of the dollar, it's clear there's no reason to have faith in the government or its money.

That's Paul's essential argument. His solution: allow competing currencies.

If individuals want to circulate gold or silver coins (or scrip backed by metal reserves), let them. Give citizens the chance to decide which money they trust.

The owners of NORFED, an Indiana coin company, gave it a shot. The company minted and sold thousands of silver Ron Paul dollars, complete with the candidate's face in profile, before federal agents showed up in November and confiscated their entire remaining inventory. In its affidavit for a search warrant, the FBI accused NORFED of trying to "undermine the United States government's financial systems by the issuance of a non-governmental competing currency for the purpose of repealing the Federal Reserve and Internal Revenue Code." That may be a crime, but it's also pretty close to Ron Paul's stump speech.

It's hard to think of a presidential candidate who's ever drawn a coalition as broad as Ron Paul's. At any Paul event, you're likely to run into self-described anarcho-capitalists, 9/11-deniers, antiwar lefties, objectivists, paleocons, hemp activists, and geeky high school kids, along with tax resisters, conspiracy nuts, and acolytes of Murray Rothbard. And those are just the ones it's possible to categorize. It's hard to say what they all have in common, except that every one is an ideological minority—or, as one of them put it to me, "open-minded people." To these supporters, Paul is a folk hero, the one person in national politics who doesn't judge them, who understands what it's like to be considered a freak by straight society.

Which is odd, because, in person, Paul doesn't seem like a freak. He seems like someone's grandfather. I first met up with Paul after a rally at University of Nevada, Las Vegas. He apparently hadn't known I was coming but accepted my arrival with Zen-like calm, welcoming me into the seat next to him in the minivan and offering me baked goods from a plate on his lap. We were both finishing our brownies when he mentioned they'd been baked by a supporter. I stopped chewing. Where I work, this is a major taboo (Rule One: Never eat food sent by viewers), and my concern must have shown. Paul grinned. "Maybe they're spiked with marijuana," he said.

If so, it would have been his first experience with illegal drugs. Though Paul argues passionately for liberalizing marijuana laws and is beloved by potheads (Timothy Leary once held a fund-raiser for him), he has never smoked pot himself. He sounded shocked when I asked him. "I have never seen anyone smoke marijuana," he said. "I don't think I'd be open to using it." For some people, libertarianism is the philosophical justification for a zany personal life. Paul, by contrast, describes his hobbies as gardening (roses and organic tomatoes) and "riding my bicycle." He has never had a cigarette. He doesn't swear. He limits his drinking to an occasional glass of wine and goes to church regularly. He has been married to the same woman for fifty years. Three of their five children are physicians.

Ron Paul is deeply square, and every bit as deeply committed to your right not to be. "I don't gamble, but I'm the gambler's best friend," he says, boasting of his support for online casinos. He is a Second Amendment absolutist who doesn't own a gun. "I've only fired one a couple of times in my life. I've never gotten around to killing anything." It's an impressively, charmingly principled worldview, though sometimes you've got to wonder how much Paul has in common with many of the people who support him.

Before we left the speech in Pahrump and headed across

the state, I'd called a friend of mine in Carson City named Dennis Hof. Dennis owns the Moonlite BunnyRanch, probably the most famous legal brothel in the country and the setting for an HBO series called *Cathouse*. Dennis isn't very political, but he's smart, and I suspected he might lean libertarian. I told him Ron Paul was speaking the next morning in Reno. He said he'd drive down to see it.

I wasn't planning on showing up at Paul's press conference with a bordello owner and two hookers, but unexpected things happen on the road.

I'd arrived with the campaign at the Best Western Airport Plaza Hotel in Reno at two in the morning the night before, and, at some point while I was sleeping, the power in the hotel went out, disabling my alarm. By the time I woke up, Paul and his staff had left. So I called Dennis for a ride. He was there in ten minutes, in an enormous stretch limo with a BunnyRanch logo on the side. He'd brought two of his girls, Brooke and Air Force Amy, as well as his driver, a middle-aged man in a cowboy hat and western wear. It was a conspicuous group.

Probably because they didn't fully understand who I was coming with, the Paul people waved the limo through a roadblock outside the auditorium and brought us in through the loading dock. A Paul aide informed us that press conferences are for press only. That's us, said the girls, and we walked right in.

The other, actual journalists looked confused. Dennis is built like a linebacker and was dressed entirely in black. Brooke and Air Force Amy looked like hookers because they are. All three slapped on Ron Paul stickers ("we could use these as pasties," Air Force Amy said, giggling) and sat near the front. Pretty soon, Paul showed up and did his fifteen minutes on liberty and Austrian economics. If he noticed there were prostitutes present, he didn't show it.

The first time I heard Paul talk about monetary policy, I'd felt like a hostage, the only person in the room who didn't buy into the program. Then, slowly, like so many hostages, I started to open my mind and listen. By the time we got to Reno, unfamiliar thoughts were beginning to occur: Why shouldn't we worry about the soundness of the currency? What exactly is the dollar backed by anyway? And, if the gold standard is crazy, is it really any crazier than hedge funds? I'd become Patty Hearst, ready to take up arms for the cause, or at least call my accountant and tell him to buy Krugerrands. I looked over at Dennis and the girls. They looked like they might be having the same thoughts.

Once the press conference ended, Paul left to do interviews with local TV reporters. Dennis and the girls stood at the podium and had their pictures taken under the Ron Paul sign. Air Force Amy hammed it up. What I really want more than anything, she told me, is to get my picture taken with Dr. Paul. She meant it.

I considered trying to explain to her that I was not actually affiliated with Ron Paul, merely writing about him for a political magazine back in Washington. But I didn't. Instead, I led all three of them into the back room where Paul was doing his interviews.

Paul was talking on camera and never saw us. But his staff

was on high alert. They looked more uncomfortable than I have ever seen a campaign staff look. Air Force Amy didn't appear to notice. Dressed in red, her Dolly Parton hairdo and 36DDs at full attention, she sidled up to Lew Moore, Paul's campaign manager, and made her pitch. "Hi," she said. "I'm Air Force Amy, and I'd like a picture with Ron Paul." I knew right away it wasn't going to happen. "I've got a concern, I've got to be honest," Moore said, tense but trying to be nice. "If that picture surfaces, it could be very damaging to him politically." Dennis stepped in to take up Air Force Amy's cause, but Moore wasn't budging. "The mainstream in the early primary states is not moving in that direction," he said.

I really thought Air Force Amy was going to cry. She looked crushed. Like a child of alcoholic parents, she immediately started to rationalize away the pain. "It wasn't Ron's decision," she told Moore. "It was yours. So I can't take it personally." But it was obvious that she did. It was awful. There wasn't much left to say, so Dennis and the girls and I left and went downtown to a casino for pancakes. There were no hard feelings. They wore their Ron Paul stickers all through breakfast. If I'd had one, I would have worn it, too.

––––––––––

More than fifteen years after his death, Hunter Thompson is probably best remembered for the way he lived: high-powered drugs, high-powered handguns, with a smoldering Dunhill in a cigarette holder clamped between his teeth. Thompson was the original outlaw journalist, a category that no longer exists. But more than anything, Thompson was a magazine writer. His stories affected an entire generation of writers, including me. By the time I finally met him, Thompson was in decline, just days as it turned out from his death. The reality of the man was sadder than expected, as it usually is. But to this day I admire his writing. I still have his pack of Dunhills in the top drawer of my desk.

"WHEN THE FUN STOPPED"

Weekly Standard, March 7, 2005

I feel like I've known Hunter S. Thompson for most of my life. I first encountered him in 1981, when I was twelve. A family friend had moved out after a long stay in the guest room, and I decided to find out what he'd left behind. On the nightstand I found a copy of _Fear and Loathing in Las Vegas._ I liked the cover art, so I read it. It changed my life.

The book made me want to drop everything (specifically, the sixth grade) and take up journalism. It made me want to travel the world with a pen and notebook, having adventures, recording my observations, and speaking fearlessly on behalf of truth as a sworn guardian of the First Amendment. But mostly, it made me want to do drugs.

In the first chapter, Thompson famously describes the stash he's accumulated for his weekend road trip to Vegas: "two bags of grass, seventy-five pellets of mescaline, five sheets of high-powered blotter acid, a saltshaker half-full of cocaine, and a whole galaxy of uppers, downers, laughers, screamers." This is in addition to "a quart of tequila, a quart of rum, a case of beer, a pint of raw ether, and two dozen amyls."

I resolved to try it all, down to the ether, which I finally located midway through tenth grade in a head shop on the West Side of Manhattan. (It gave me double vision and a headache.) Tracking down and taking everything on Thompson's list became a kind of mission, a pharmacological scavenger hunt that preoccupied me through high school.

At this point, I should add the customary disclaimer about how drugs are bad, a lie and a trap and a destroyer of lives. That's all true, but not in my case. For me, the whole experience was interesting and fun. I had a great time.

On the other hand, I grew out of it. By the time I got to college, mind expansion had lost its appeal. I switched to beer.

One night in freshman year, I drove to Providence to see Hunter Thompson debate G. Gordon Liddy in a lecture hall at Brown. Thompson showed up slobbering, then got even drunker. He took swigs from a bottle of whiskey and yelled incoherently about Richard Nixon. But booze wasn't the basic problem. Dead sober, Thompson still would have embarrassed himself. He didn't have much to say.

Later I learned that every childhood hero disappoints you if you get close enough. But that night at Brown, I was stunned, and totally disillusioned. Thompson wasn't anything like I'd imagined.

It was eighteen years before I saw him again. Last month,

a friend invited my wife and me to New Orleans to have dinner with Hunter Thompson. We met at Arnaud's in the French Quarter. Thompson couldn't make it to the second floor dining room because of a bad leg, so we sat at the bar. He didn't say much, and when he did he spoke in a faint, slurry voice. He smiled a lot. He could not have been nicer.

I wasn't shocked this time, just sad. For a while, Thompson was the funniest writer in America. His sentences were tight and precise and perfectly balanced. Now he seemed almost unable to communicate with words.

After an hour or so, I got up to leave. Rather than shake my hand, Thompson leaned forward and pulled me in, hugging me so hard and for so long that his lapel pin left an imprint on my check. Then he handed me his pack of Dunhills, Superior Mild, with one left in the box. I couldn't tell if he wanted me to smoke the cigarette, or if he was passing it on as a keepsake. I put the pack in my pocket. It's sitting on my desk as I type.

The night after Hunter Thompson killed himself I got into bed with my copy of *Fear and Loathing in Las Vegas*. I finished it at dawn. I'm happy to say I wasn't disappointed. It was as good as I remembered.

Even by the standards of boys, I was an unusually lazy child. Indolence was effectively my religion. Before the age of nineteen, I can't remember a single moment in which I enjoyed working at anything. That changed in a single summer. I went to work on the second shift at a baked bean factory in Maine. Suddenly labor made sense. Work gives order and meaning to your life. Accomplishment makes you feel good, even when it's just eight hours of adding barbecue flavor to cast iron pots. I loved the whole thing, though to this day I still can't eat baked beans.

"EAT, MEMORY: BEAN THERE"

New York Times, March 26, 2006

I bet we were the only people in my neighborhood growing up who ate B&M baked beans. We lived in La Jolla, California, thirty miles north of the Mexican border, where the only beans you saw were refried or served in salad. B&M beans came in a can, suspended in molasses with a chunk of salt pork. They seemed like the sort of thing you'd eat by the woodstove if you were snowbound in the mountains. They were a little heavy for La Jolla.

That was doubtless the appeal for my father, who came from New England and ate things like shepherd's pie, rhubarb, and other mysterious foods that baffled guacamole-stuffed Southern California natives like my brother and me. But we ate the beans anyway, partly out of respect for my father, but also because they were delicious. In the summers, on the way from the Boston airport to vacation in Maine, we'd salute as we drove past the immense brick B&M plant in Portland. I remember wondering who worked there.

One summer during college, I found out. My roommate and I were living in Portland, though not very successfully. I'd applied to Denny's; he'd put his name in for a bartending job. Neither of us heard back. We sold car insurance door-to-door for a day. Finally we tried a temp agency. The next afternoon we found ourselves wearing white uniforms and hairnets and reporting for duty at the Burnham & Morrill baked-bean factory.

B&M was a strict union shop, closed to all but members of the Bakery, Confectionery, Tobacco Workers and Grain Millers International, local 334, and possibly their sons and nephews. But for some reason that summer the union allowed an exemption for temporary help. We went to work on the second shift at $6.60 an hour.

The B&M plant was built in 1913 and, from what I could tell, hadn't been updated since. Outside, the building was dominated by a towering brick smokestack that belched bean fumes into the salty Portland air. Inside, it was a time capsule. True to advertising, B&M's beans (white pea and red kidney) were cooked as they had always been, in enormous cast-iron pots that were lowered into brick ovens. The pots hung from chains and moved across the plant floor on steel rails suspended from the ceiling.

It looked to me as if someone must have bribed the safety inspectors. Each bean pot was the size of a Fiat. They whipped across the floor at surprisingly high speeds, often pushed by workers who looked as if they could have used a nap. (When your shift starts at four in the afternoon, there's ample time to drink before work.) Occasionally a pot would slip the rails and come crashing down. I saw it happen once. The impact sounded like a massive explosion. During our next smoke break, one of my gossiping coworkers claimed that the Burnham & Morrill plant had the highest rate of work-related injuries in all of Pet Inc., then the corporate parent. I believed him.

Most of my jobs were safe enough. One week I scraped charred beans from the insides of the ovens. The next I ran a machine that stacked cans onto pallets. For two weeks after that, I extracted the hot cans in which B&M baked its brown bread. They were made in enormous pressure cookers that looked like missile silos and were called reefers, for some mysterious reason. By the end, I got curious about the bread and tasted some. Surprisingly, it was pretty good.

By July I'd been assigned to a pot-saucing station, mixing ingredients for 16- and 18-ounce containers of barbecue-flavored pea beans. For each pot we combined 21 gallons of hot water with 4.3 ounces of mustard slurry, a portion of ground bacon, and 8 ounces of liquid hickory-smoke flavor. I was the liquid-hickory man.

Until that day, I'd naively imagined that food ingredients resembled food. Not so with barbecue sauce (that is, liquid-hickory flavor). The flavor came in white plastic fifty-gallon drums, shipped from a chemical plant in New Jersey. I learned right away that you didn't want to get the flavoring on your skin. It was the consistency of oil-based deck sealant and harder to remove. Within an hour every one of my fingers was dyed a deep yellow, the color of nicotine stains. I looked like a wino with a bad Pall Mall habit.

But at least I wasn't bored. The women on the pork line clearly were. I walked by them several times a day as they stood silently at a conveyor belt, dropping pieces of salt pork into cans of beans, one piece per can, eight hours a day. The monotony was enough to make you hope for a falling bean pot.

One day toward the end of my short career at the plant, a supervisor sent me to a storeroom on the third floor. Inside there was a pile of hundreds of bean cans, all of them full. Apparently some of these cans had bad seams. It was impossible to know exactly which ones were defective, but the company wasn't taking chances. Leaky seams meant spoiled product, maybe even botulism. You couldn't just throw them away, for fear that someone would retrieve them from the trash, eat them, get sick, and sue. They had to be destroyed. My job was simple: puncture every can.

The assignment came with a special tool, fabricated in the millwright's shop. It looked like a framing hammer with a steel spike welded to the end. It made a satisfying sound as it pierced the cans.

I had a great time for the first hour. Then I came to a bad can. I should have known what it was. It looked different than the others, misshapen and bulging in the middle. If you've ever shot a can of shaving cream with a BB gun, you know what happened next. A plume of fermented beans burst forth like a geyser. The liquid was brown and bubbling and smelled like sewer gas. It hit me directly in the face, spraying into my eyes and mouth, and running down the inside of my collar. I felt like screaming, but there were people watching, so I just kept whacking cans. My uniform stuck to me for the rest of the night.

On my final day of work, I stopped by the company store to pick up some beans, which B&M sold to employees at cost. Cheap beans were considered a key perk of the job, and in fact they were. The labels were often flawed and the cans dented, but the beans were fine, and incredibly inexpensive. For three dollars, I bought a case of pork-free pea beans in sauce. I threw it on the backseat of my car and drove off.

Last year I was rooting through a cabinet in the laundry room of our summer house looking for Fourth of July fireworks. There, next to a leaky container of Tide, were the beans. I'd bought them fully intending to cook them for dinner. Tastes change over time, though. I worked there in 1989. I haven't had a baked bean since.

———

Hardly anyone remembers old Bob Smith of New Hampshire. Smith was one of countless U.S. senators through the years who've convinced themselves they're going to be president. That never happened. But I remember him well. I admired Bob Smith. He was the least cynical man in Washington. Needless to say, Smith didn't last long. God knows where he is now. In this piece, I believe I caught Smith at his apogee.

"MR. SMITH GOES
THIRD PARTY"

Weekly Standard, July 26, 1999

I'm going to be president of the United States," Senator Bob
Smith of New Hampshire says in a perfectly even voice. "I
really believe that."

It's not a majority view. Two weeks ago, only Smith, his
family, and selected political science professors seemed to know
he was running for president. He was polling twelfth among
the twelve announced Republican candidates; only one percent
of the voters in his own state said they planned to vote for him.
Things looked grim for Smith 2000. Then, last week, Smith
announced he was leaving the Republican Party and becoming
an Independent. Instantly, the electoral calculus changed. Bob
Smith may have been last among Republicans, but in the field of
third-party candidates, he is indisputably Number One.

Of course, depending on how you count, Smith may also be the only third-party candidate in the presidential race. Not that it makes any difference to him. The point is, Smith explains from his office in the Dirksen Building, people are excited about the possibility of a Smith administration. "Without exaggeration, we've received five thousand pledges of support," he says. "They've come from Republicans, Democrats, Independents. It's unbelievable. We're not equipped to handle it." Smith pauses, allowing time for the sheer size of the political tsunami to sink in. No reporter, he recognizes, should have to take news like this at face value. "You probably think I'm trying to game you," he says understandingly. "But I'm not."

Smith doesn't seem like the kind of politician who goes around gaming people. Rather, he seems perpetually gamed, the sort of person for whom life's unpleasant realities dawn slowly and hard. You get the feeling Smith was the last kid on his block to learn the truth about Santa Claus.

He was almost certainly the last person in Washington to discover that the Republican platform is irrelevant to actual politics. Smith was outraged when he found out. "The Republican platform," he declared in his party-switching speech to the Senate, "is a meaningless document that has been put out there so that suckers like me and maybe suckers like you out there can read it."

Smith's speech went on like this for close to an hour. Through all of it, he howled like a man deceived, the lone member of the Senate Sucker Caucus. He even read portions of the platform aloud. It was a mean thing to do—as close to a dirty trick as Smith is probably capable of—but instructive nonetheless. "As a first step in reforming government," Smith thundered, reciting the painfully hopeful words of some unnamed party scribe, "we support elimination of the Departments of Commerce, Housing and Urban Development, Education, and Energy." Whatever happened to that promise? he demanded. Or to the promise to defund Legal Services? Not to mention public broadcasting, the UN, and the National Endowment for the Arts. And where's the legislation that would "make clear that the Fourteenth Amendment's protections apply to unborn children"? After five and a half years of Republican control of Congress, Smith wanted to know, where is any of it?

It's easy to sympathize with Smith. (Imagine if you woke up one morning after ten years in office and found politics in your political party.) It's harder to understand how he made it all the way to the U.S. Senate, much less how he'll mount a credible presidential campaign. For the moment, though, several of the other Republican candidates appear to view Smith as useful. Before Smith had even announced his defection, Gary Bauer and Dan Quayle chimed in to say they could understand the senator's frustration with the unprincipled, lemming-like (read: George W. Bush–supporting) Republican Establishment. "We are the party of middle America, not the party of the country club," explained Quayle, who grew up on a golf course.

The idea seems to be that Smith's attacks on Republican moderates will call attention to Bush's fundamentally moderate positions on social issues, thereby energizing the fabled Republican Base. Once energized, the Base will recognize Bush for the Rockefeller Republican he is, and support other, more conservative candidates. In the end, the reasoning goes, Bush may still win, but he'll have to act more conservative to do so. "The Smith thing," says Bauer strategist Jeff Bell, "underscores what Gary has been saying all along, which is that there is going to be a contest."

It's not a totally crackpot theory. Smith will probably join the U.S. Taxpayers Party, which is already on the ballot in several states. (The likelihood he'll sign up with the much larger Reform Party diminished when Jesse Ventura didn't return his call.) And Smith's defection could increase the leverage of the remaining challengers to Bush. In any event, he won't need much money to run—Smith is happy to drive himself to events—and he seems deadly serious about staying in till November 2000. And if Bush is the nominee, Smith is betting that, as a third-party candidate, he can pick up the support Bush's failed conservative challengers have left behind.

Every candidate, of course, has a Scenario, the sometimes Rube Goldberg–like series of events that, if executed in sequence, leads to victory. Strategists at the George W. Bush campaign aren't impressed with Smith's. They have no snappy explanation for why Smith doesn't matter. They don't even bother to scoff. Bob who?

Smith seems ready for this. He knows there will always be some who will dismiss his campaign as a mere curiosity. "Some people view it as not even serious," Smith says in a tone that suggests he's passing on a secret. Then again, some people haven't seen the mail that has poured into Smith's office over the past few days. The mail that says Bob Smith of New Hampshire is going to be the next president of the United States. The mail that Smith fervently, wholeheartedly believes. "I think young people are going to be joining this campaign by the millions," he says. "I feel very confident about this. I'm absolutely convinced I can win. I wouldn't do it if I wasn't."

Smith pauses again. He's caught himself gloating. "I'm not trying to boast," he says, almost embarrassed. "I'm just trying to tell you what I think we can do."

———

Unlike Bob Smith, Mike Forbes was a far more recognizable sort of politician, the kind who'd do anything to serve his own interests. Find a greasy pole, and Mike Forbes would be happy to climb it. In the end, Forbes didn't get far. He was too cynical even for politics. I remember him mostly because I so deeply enjoyed writing the first three sentences of this story, which were relayed to me by several Mike Forbes staffers who despised him.

"A NEW DEMOCRAT"

Weekly Standard, August 2, 1999

Mike Forbes likes soup. But he doesn't like corn. So when Forbes, a third-term congressman from New York, found corn in his dehydrated soup-in-a-cup, he had a member of his congressional staff remove every kernel.

Picking corn out of soup is a tedious task, even by the standards of Capitol Hill, but members of Forbes's staff were used to such assignments. Many had already seen the congressman explode after an aide was slow to wash a dirty cereal bowl Forbes had left in a sink. Others had heard about the time Forbes lost his temper when a female assistant forgot to drain the water from his canned tuna before serving it to him.

Forbes has never been an easy man to work for. Over the course of his first four and a half years in Congress, a total of fifty-three staffers resigned or were fired from his office, a rate of about one a month. Then, two weeks ago, Forbes announced he was leaving the Republican Party and becoming a Democrat. Every member of his staff immediately quit. Many say they are happy to be looking for new jobs. "He's a screamer," says one. "I was afraid of him," says Tina Mufford, his former staff assistant, "afraid he'd go off."

Not afraid he'd go off and become a Democrat, though. Virtually no one in Forbes's office anticipated that. Late in the afternoon of July 16, Forbes, still a Republican, left the Capitol and drove with a member of his staff to Reagan National Airport outside Washington. When he got to the airport, Forbes drove past the terminals and into the private airfield next door. His aide, legislative director Brian Fauls, was confused. "I asked him what he was doing," Fauls remembers. "He said, 'I'm bumming a ride from someone.'" As Fauls discovered later, the "someone" turned out to be the Democratic Congressional Campaign Committee, which had sent a Learjet to take Forbes home to Long Island.

Forbes landed in New York and was picked up by a member of his district staff. Forbes and a DCCC operative sat in the back of the car talking. Forbes's driver listened, stunned, as the two chatted about Forbes's new party affiliation. At one point, Forbes fretted about his wife, Barbara, a staunch Republican who once worked at the Bush White House. "Barbara's still not sure about this," Forbes said. "You may have to help me convince her."

The driver dropped Forbes at his house and immediately called the staff at the Washington office to pass on what he had heard. Forbes himself called several hours later. The next day he held a press conference to tell the world. Ordinarily, Forbes's switch would have made the evening news. Unfortunately for him, Forbes chose to become a Democrat on the same day John Kennedy Jr.'s plane went down. The competition for coverage irritated Forbes. "This is really going to hurt my press," he told his executive assistant, Jeff LaCourse.

In his statement, Forbes complained, "There's no room in the Republican Party in Congress for moderates like myself." The only problem is, Forbes was never a moderate. A pro-life, pro-gun member of the famously ferocious freshman class of 1994, Forbes voted for all four counts of impeachment against President Clinton. Each January, he held a reception in his Washington office for antiabortion protesters commemorating the anniversary of *Roe v. Wade*. This spring, he endorsed George W. Bush for president.

Forbes has since suggested that his endorsement of Bush was less than wholehearted, and it probably was. Forbes originally planned to back Senator John McCain in the presidential race. Earlier this year, he had discussions with McCain strategists, even floated the possibility of giving stump speeches on McCain's behalf. Then Al D'Amato called. Forbes once worked for D'Amato, and has remained in close contact with the former New York senator. According to LaCourse, "D'Amato told him, 'You're going to endorse Bush, and that's all there is to it.'" Forbes, who by all accounts is afraid of D'Amato, grudgingly agreed. "We paid the price for it," says LaCourse. "He was in a bad mood for a week."

Forbes won't have to take calls from Al D'Amato anymore.

But he still hasn't retracted his endorsement of George W. Bush. Nor, apart from the usual talking points about Republican extremism, has he explained why, exactly, he switched parties. A high-level Democratic staffer who has spoken extensively with Forbes says two events pushed him over the edge. First was a speech that Representative Tom DeLay gave shortly after the shootings at Columbine High School. In it, DeLay seemed to blame day-care programs for producing a generation of violent children. "That upset Forbes a great deal," says the staffer, "especially since his own kids had been through day care. He thought it was out of touch." The second event occurred just four days before Forbes switched parties, when Republicans sponsored a nonbinding resolution condemning sexual relations between adults and children. Like just about everyone else in the House, Forbes voted for the resolution. At the same time, explains the Democratic staffer, he was disgusted by Republican grandstanding. "He said, 'Of course [pedophilia] is bad. But should we really be talking about this?'"

LaCourse remembers Forbes's reaction differently. The pedophilia vote was held on a Monday, which forced Forbes to return to Washington earlier than usual. Forbes was infuriated by the time he got to Washington, yelling at his chief of staff when he arrived. "He's very lazy," says LaCourse. "He just hated coming in."

After this fall, Forbes may never have to come in again. His district—mostly Suffolk Country, at the Hamptons end of Long Island—is largely Republican. By switching parties, Forbes has guaranteed himself a tough general election race. But he may also face a primary challenge. For months, Tony Bullock, the forty-two-year-old chief of staff to retiring New York senator Daniel Patrick Moynihan, has been mulling a run for Forbes's seat. Bullock held various elected offices in the district for more than a decade, beginning in 1983. He is smart and well connected, and he loathes Mike Forbes. "Intellectually, he's a lightweight," Bullock says. "He's a person with very little basic decency."

Worse, Bullock claims, Forbes is still a conservative. "Mike Forbes is pro-life, pro-impeachment, pro–assault weapon, pro-Bush," Bullock says. "My phone has practically melted the past few days from Suffolk County Democrats calling to say, 'My God. I'm not going to work for this guy. I'm not going to vote for him.'" Party strategists at the DCCC, Bullock claims, didn't learn anything about the politics of the district before encouraging Forbes to become a Democrat. "The geniuses who thought this up should have done the research," Bullock says. Instead, "they may have gone to the Hamptons once for the weekend. . . . They're running a dead animal for this slot."

Staff at the DCCC, meanwhile, dismiss Bullock as a malcontent who will never find the courage to challenge Forbes. Bullock may or may not run, but some of his points are harder to dismiss. How, for instance, will the state party run Forbes alongside its presumed Senate candidate, Hillary Clinton? "How can he stand there next to Mrs. Clinton," Bullock asks, "with his George W. Bush pin and his pro-life record?" And how will Forbes explain away his long association with Dov Hikind, the hotheaded Brooklyn assemblyman who has repeatedly denounced Mrs. Clinton for her "love affair with Yasser Arafat"?

It's not clear that Forbes thought about any of this before he took the plunge. None of his former staffers seems to have any idea why he switched parties, though many mention that he had been acting odder than usual in recent months. "He's bipolar," says one. "I think the clinical term is manic-depressive," says Jeff LaCourse. "All his behavior is weird. This is just the culmination of it."

Tony Bullock has never worked for Forbes, but he sees the same pattern. "It's a desperate act of self-immolation," Bullock says. "He's a few fries short of a Happy Meal."

———————

Most of the people I knew in Washington were baffled and enraged by Donald Trump. I never felt that way. Trump himself could be ridiculous, but the movement he led always made sense to me. It was a reaction against the stupidity and obtuseness of American politics, a status quo that clearly couldn't continue. By the beginning of 2016, it seemed obvious that Trump could win the nomination and be president. I wanted to predict that in print before it happened, so I wrote this in a single sitting, banging away on my iPad in my kitchen in Washington, reading passages aloud to my wife, who because she's a nice person nodded in agreement. Why did I publish the story in Politico? *Honestly, I can't remember why. Whatever the reason, I regret it. Politico is garbage, though I'm glad they ran this. It turned out to be right.*

"DONALD TRUMP IS SHOCKING, VULGAR, AND RIGHT"

Politico Magazine, January 28, 2016

About fifteen years ago, I said something nasty on CNN about Donald Trump's hair. I can't now remember the context, assuming there was one. In any case, Trump saw it and left a message the next day.

"It's true you have better hair than I do," Trump said matter-of-factly. "But I get more pussy than you do." Click.

At the time, I'd never met Trump and I remember feeling amused but also surprised he'd say something like that. Now the pattern seems entirely familiar. The message had all the earmarks of a Trump attack: shocking, vulgar, and indisputably true.

Not everyone finds it funny. On my street in Northwest Washington, D.C., there's never been anyone as unpopular as

Trump. The Democrats assume he's a bigot, pandering to the morons out there in the great dark space between Georgetown and Brentwood. The Republicans (those relatively few who live here) fully agree with that assessment, and they hate him even more. They sense Trump is a threat to them personally, to their legitimacy and their livelihoods. Idi Amin would get a warmer reception in our dog park.

I understand it, of course. And, except in those moments when the self-righteous silliness of rich people overwhelms me and I feel like moving to Maine, I can see their points, some of them anyway. Trump might not be my first choice for president. I'm not even convinced he really wants the job. He's smart enough to know it would be tough for him to govern.

But just because Trump is an imperfect candidate doesn't mean his candidacy can't be instructive. Trump could teach Republicans in Washington a lot if only they stopped posturing long enough to watch carefully. Here's some of what they might learn:

He Exists Because You Failed

American presidential elections usually amount to a series of overcorrections: Clinton begat Bush, who produced Obama, whose lax border policies fueled the rise of Trump. In the case of Trump, though, the GOP shares the blame, and not just because his fellow Republicans misdirected their ad buys or waited so long to criticize him. Trump is in part a reaction to the intellectual corruption of the Republican Party. That ought to be obvious to his critics, yet somehow it isn't.

Consider the conservative nonprofit establishment, which seems to employ most right-of-center adults in Washington. Over the past forty years, how much donated money have all those think tanks and foundations consumed? Billions, certainly. (Someone better at math and less prone to melancholy should probably figure out the precise number.) Has America become more conservative over that same period? Come on. Most of that cash went to self-perpetuation: salaries, bonuses, retirement funds, medical, dental, lunches, car services, leases on high-end office space, retreats in Mexico, more fund-raising. Unless you were the direct beneficiary of any of that, you'd have to consider it wasted.

Pretty embarrassing. And yet they're not embarrassed. Many of those same overpaid, underperforming tax-exempt sinecure-holders are now demanding that Trump be stopped. Why? Because, as his critics have noted in a rising chorus of hysteria, Trump represents "an existential threat to conservatism."

Let that sink in. Conservative voters are being scolded for supporting a candidate they consider conservative because it would be bad for conservatism? And by the way, the people doing the scolding? They're the ones who've been advocating for open borders, and nation-building in countries whose populations hate us, and trade deals that eliminated jobs while enriching their donors, all while implicitly mocking the base for its worries about abortion and gay marriage and the pace of demographic change. Now they're telling their voters to shut up and obey, and if they don't, they're liberal.

It turns out the GOP wasn't simply out of touch with its

voters; the party had no idea who its voters were or what they believed. For decades, party leaders and intellectuals imagined that most Republicans were broadly libertarian on economics and basically neoconservative on foreign policy. That may sound absurd now, after Trump has attacked nearly the entire Republican catechism (he savaged the Iraq War and hedge fund managers in the same debate) and been greatly rewarded for it, but that was the assumption the GOP brain trust operated under. They had no way of knowing otherwise. The only Republicans they talked to read the *Wall Street Journal,* too.

On immigration policy, party elders were caught completely by surprise. Even canny operators like Ted Cruz didn't appreciate the depth of voter anger on the subject. And why would they? If you live in an affluent ZIP code, it's hard to see a downside to mass low-wage immigration. Your kids don't go to public school. You don't take the bus or use the emergency room for health care. No immigrant is competing for your job. (The day Hondurans start getting hired as green energy lobbyists is the day my neighbors become nativists.) Plus, you get cheap servants, and get to feel welcoming and virtuous while paying them less per hour than your kids make at a summer job on Nantucket. It's all good.

Apart from his line about Mexican rapists early in the campaign, Trump hasn't said anything especially shocking about immigration. Control the border, deport lawbreakers, try not to admit violent criminals—these are the ravings of a Nazi? This is the "ghost of George Wallace" that a *Politico* piece described last August? A lot of Republican leaders think so. No wonder their voters are rebelling.

97

Truth Is Not Only a Defense, It's Thrilling

When was the last time you stopped yourself from saying something you believed to be true for fear of being punished or criticized for saying it? If you live in America, it probably hasn't been long. That's not just a talking point about political correctness. It's the central problem with our national conversation, the main reason our debates are so stilted and useless. You can't fix a problem if you don't have the words to describe it. You can't even think about it clearly.

This depressing fact made Trump's political career. In a country where almost everyone in public life lies reflexively, it's thrilling to hear someone say what he really thinks, even if you believe he's wrong. It's especially exciting when you suspect he's right.

A temporary ban on Muslim immigration? That sounds a little extreme (meaning nobody else has said it recently in public). But is it? Millions of Muslims have moved to Western Europe over the past fifty years, and a sizable number of them still haven't assimilated. Instead, they remain hostile and sometimes dangerous to the cultures that welcomed them. By any measure, that experiment has failed. What's our strategy for not repeating it here, especially after San Bernardino—attacks that seemed to come out of nowhere? Invoke American exceptionalism and hope for the best? Before Trump, that was the plan.

Republican primary voters should be forgiven for wondering who exactly is on the reckless side of this debate. At the very least, Trump seems like he wants to protect the country.

Evangelicals understand this better than most. You read surveys that indicate the majority of Christian conservatives support Trump, and then you see the video: Trump onstage with pastors, looking pained as they pray over him, misidentifying key books in the New Testament, and in general doing a ludicrous imitation of a faithful Christian, the least holy roller ever. You wonder as you watch this: How could they be that dumb? He's so obviously faking it.

They know that already. I doubt there are many Christian voters who think Trump could recite the Nicene Creed, or even identify it. Evangelicals have given up trying to elect one of their own. What they're looking for is a bodyguard, someone to shield them from mounting (and real) threats to their freedom of speech and worship. Trump fits that role nicely, better in fact than many churchgoing Republicans. For eight years, there was a born-again in the White House. How'd that work out for Christians, here and in Iraq?

Washington Really Is Corrupt

Everyone beats up on Washington, but most of the people I know who live here love it. Of course they do. It's beautiful, the people are friendly, we've got good restaurants, not to mention full employment and construction cranes on virtually every corner. If you work on Capitol Hill or downtown, it's hard to walk back from lunch without seeing someone you know. It's a warm bath. Nobody wants to leave.

But let's pretend for a second this isn't Washington. Let's

imagine it's the capital of an African country, say Burkina Faso, and we are doing a study on corruption. Probably the first question we'd ask: How many government officials have close relatives who make a living by influencing government spending? A huge percentage of them? Okay. Case closed. Ouagadougou is obviously a very corrupt city.

That's how the rest of the country views D.C. Washington is probably the richest city in America because the people who live there have the closest proximity to power. That seems obvious to most voters. It's less obvious to us, because everyone here is so cheerful and familiar, and we're too close to it. Chairman so-and-so's son-in-law lobbies the committee? That doesn't seem corrupt. He's such a good guy.

All of which explains why almost nobody in Washington caught the significance of Trump's finest moment in the first debate. One of the moderators asked, in effect: if you're so opposed to Hillary Clinton, why did she come to your last wedding? It seemed like a revealing, even devastating question.

Trump's response, delivered without pause or embarrassment: because I paid her to be there. As if she was the wedding singer, or in charge of the catering.

Even then, I'll confess, I didn't get it. (Why would you pay someone to come to your wedding?) But the audience did. Trump is the ideal candidate to fight Washington corruption not simply because he opposes it, but because he has personally participated in it. He's not just a reformer; like most effective populists, he's a whistle-blower, a traitor to his class. Before he became the most ferocious enemy American business had ever known, Teddy Roosevelt was a rich guy. His privilege wasn't incidental; it was key to his appeal. Anyone can peer through the window in envy. It takes a real man to throw furniture through it from the inside.

If Trump is leading a populist movement, many of his Republican critics have joined an elitist one. Deriding Trump is an act of class solidarity, visible evidence of refinement and proof that you live nowhere near a Wal-Mart. Early last summer, in a piece that greeted Trump when he entered the race, *National Review* described the candidate as "a ridiculous buffoon with the worst taste since Caligula." Virtually every other critique of Trump from the right has voiced similar aesthetic concerns.

Why is the Party of Ideas suddenly so fixated on fashion and hair? Maybe all dying institutions devolve this way, from an insistence on intellectual rigor to a flabby preoccupation with appearances. It happened in the Episcopal Church, once renowned for its liturgy, now a stop on architectural and garden tours. Only tourists go there anymore.

He Could Win

Of all the dumb things that have been said about Trump by people who were too slow to get finance jobs and therefore wound up in journalism, perhaps the stupidest of all is the one you hear most: He'll get killed in the general! This is a godsend for Democrats! Forty-state wipeout! And so it goes mindlessly on.

Actually—and this is no endorsement of Trump, just an interjection of reality—that's a crock. Of the Republicans now running, Trump likely has the best chance to beat Hillary Clinton, for two reasons:

First, he's the only Republican who can meaningfully expand the pie. Polls show a surprisingly large number of Democrats open to Trump. In one *January survey* by the polling firm Mercury Analytics, almost 20 percent said they'd consider crossing over to him from Hillary. Even if that's double the actual number, it's still stunning. Could Ted Cruz expect to draw that many Democrats? Could Jeb?

It's an article of faith in Washington that Trump would tank the party's prospects with minority voters. Sounds logical, especially if you're a sensitive white liberal who considers the suggestion of a border wall a form of hate speech, but consider the baseline. In the last election, Romney got 6 percent of the black vote, and 27 percent of Hispanics. Trump, who's energetic, witty, and successful, will do worse? I wouldn't bet on it.

But the main reason Trump could win is that he's the only candidate hard enough to call Hillary's bluff. Republicans will say almost anything about Hillary, but almost none challenge her basic competence. She may be evil, but she's tough and accomplished. This we know, all of us.

But do we? Or is this understanding of Hillary just another piety we repeat out of unthinking habit, the political equivalent of "you can be whatever you want to be" or "breakfast is the most important meal of the day"? Trump doesn't think Hillary is impressive and strong. He sees her as brittle and afraid.

He may be right, based on his exchange with her just before Christmas. During a speech in Grand Rapids, Michigan, Trump said Hillary had been "schlonged" by Obama in the 2008 race. In response, the Clinton campaign called Trump a sexist. It's a charge Hillary has leveled against virtually every opponent she's faced, but Trump responded differently. Instead of scrambling to donate to breast cancer research, he pointed out that Hillary spent years attacking the alleged victims of her husband's sexual assaults. That ended the conversation almost immediately.

It was the most effective possible response, though more obvious than brilliant. Why was Trump the only Republican to use it?

Republican primary voters may be wondering the same thing. Or maybe they already know. They seem to know a lot about Trump, more than the people who run their party. They know that he isn't a conventional ideological conservative. They seem relieved. They can see that he's emotionally incontinent. They find it exciting.

Washington Republicans look on at this in horror, their suspicions confirmed. Beneath the thin topsoil of rural conservatism, they see the seeds of proto-fascism beginning to sprout. But that's not quite right. Republicans in the states aren't dangerous. They've just evaluated the alternatives and decided those are worse.

It's hard to retaliate against the people who flood your email account with spam. Twenty-five years ago, it was easier. Telemarketers had to call your house. You got to talk to them directly. If you were feeling creative, you could exact revenge for interrupting your dinner. It became one of my favorite hobbies.

"THE UNFLAPPABLES"

Weekly Standard, December 25, 1995

Most people get annoyed when salesmen call during dinner. Not at my house. We love it. A call from somebody hawking burial plots or new long-distance service may interrupt the meal, but it also gives us a chance to play Scare the Solicitor, my family's favorite parlor game. The object is to say something so disturbing, so bizarre, to a telemarketer that he'll never call again, maybe even give up phone sales for good. It's harder than it sounds.

"Hi, Mr. Carlson, this is Brandon Mink, from Merrill Lynch."

"Hi." (Voice sounds kind of familiar. Do I know this guy?)

"Mr. Carlson, if you have a second, I'd like to talk to you about some important investment opportunities."

"Well, to tell you the truth, Brandon, I can't. I'm kind of busy. I'm having my other leg amputated in the morning. Got to pack for the hospital."

(Pause. Nervous chuckle.) "You're kidding, right?"

"Unfortunately not." (Did he just ask me if I was kidding?) "Had the other one taken off last year. Terrible experience. Just when I was getting used to one prosthesis, they're getting me another. I'm not looking forward to it."

"Wow. Sorry. Well, listen, would you have time to talk when you get out?"

"Actually, Brandon, I'm going out of town after I leave the hospital. Headed up to Minnesota for a couple of months. Going to get some experimental therapy, see if I'll ever walk again. I won't be back till March."

"Hmm. Okay. Well, maybe I could call you then. Will you be at this number?"

Sound callous? Not by the standards of the people who call my house. (Though, to be fair, Brandon from Merrill Lynch did write a follow-up note a few days later. "If your spirits stay high," he wrote in ballpoint at the bottom of the investment pitch, "you'll never be low.")

Just the other night, Sherri from Rollins Protective Services dialed up to see if I wanted to buy some fantastically expensive alarm system. So I told her I was blind.

"Legally blind?" she asked. "Oh, totally blind," I said. "I was young, a chemistry set blew up in my face."

From across the room my wife grimaced, as if to say I was going too far.

Which I was, but then so was Sherri.

"Well, we have a model for the visually impaired," Sherri offered hopefully. "It doesn't have Braille, but the buttons are raised. Alarms are especially important for the handicapped." She didn't miss a beat. "If your house caught fire, the alarm would wake you up and the fire department would come and lead you outside."

She almost had me. "I'm not sure," I said. "I have this terrible drinking problem. I don't think I'd wake up even if the alarm went off." "Well," she countered, "the firemen would just carry you out."

Clearly nothing was going to deter this woman. Finally, in a desperate move, I slammed the handset against the wall, made a yelping sound and muttered something about hitting my head on a kitchen cabinet. "Got to go," I said.

But she ignored me. "Could I at least come over and show it to you?" she pleaded. "Show it to me?" I harrumphed with what was rapidly becoming real indignation. "I'm blind."

Over the years, I've tried just about every disease and physical deformity I could think of on phone solicitors, the whole gamut from kidney dialysis and advanced melanoma to more esoteric maladies like lupus and Hansen's disease. When Greenpeace canvassers would show up at our door begging for money, I'd stare at them in bovine incomprehension without saying a word. Taking their clipboard, I'd write, "I am a deaf-mute" in big, scrawly letters and keep staring. Usually, they'd get uncomfortable and leave quickly (though one patient volunteer spent ten minutes trying to explain acid rain to me in hand gestures).

But all of these were just short-term solutions. What I really needed was something to scare them off for good, some way to get blacklisted by phone salesmen. By the time Citibank called last summer hoping to hook me on a new credit bargain, I thought I had it all figured out.

"Would you like to take advantage of our new Credit Value Plus Voucher Savings Plan today?" the woman asked.

"Of course, I'd love to," I said. "But I don't know if I should. My future's kind of up in the air at this point. I'd better wait to find out what happens with my appeal."

"Your appeal?"

"Yeah, I'm out on bond right now. Maybe you read about it—I killed three people in a drug-related murder spree a couple of years ago. I'm out now trying to beat the charges. And it's expensive. You wouldn't believe what lawyers cost. So I really don't think I should take advantage of the offer till I win my case."

"I know you're innocent," she said perkily.

"I'm not. I definitely did it. But I'll probably get off anyway. This is America."

"Good luck!" she said.

It's hard to believe that something as historically discredited and morally grotesque as eugenics still exists in this country, but it does. In fact, it's less constrained than ever. This story is as shocking to me now as it was the day I wrote it. The sad thing is, I remember believing the story might make a difference. The second people hear about this, I thought, they'll be outraged. They'll do something to stop it. But they weren't, and they didn't. I'm not sure what the lesson from that is, but it's a depressing one.

"EUGENICS, AMERICAN STYLE"

Weekly Standard, December 1, 1996

Testifying before Congress in the spring of 1990, Arkansas state health director Joycelyn Elders took an unusual tack in her defense of legal abortion. "Abortion," she said, "has had an important, and positive, public-health effect," in that it has reduced "the number of children afflicted with severe defects." As evidence, the future surgeon general cited this statistic: "The number of Down's Syndrome infants in Washington state in 1976 was 64 percent lower than it would have been without legal abortion."

Her remark went all but unnoticed at the time and has received little attention since, even during Elders's contentious tenure as surgeon general in the Clinton administration. But it was a significant statement nonetheless, if only because it represents one of the few occasions on which a public health official has publicly acknowledged the eugenic utility of abortion.

Terminating a pregnancy, Elders argued, is not simply a difficult personal decision, an agonizing last resort. When guided by public-health objectives, abortion can also be a positive act—a means of improving the species.

Stylized and dulled by euphemism as it is, the debate over abortion in America rarely allows for statements as clear and direct as Elders's, and the words may sound almost unrecognizably harsh to ears accustomed to intentionally opaque terms such as "choice" and "life." But what Elders said is nothing new. For thirty years, nearly every element of Western medicine—physicians, geneticists, insurance companies—has, explicitly and not, encouraged the use of abortion to reduce the incidence of birth defects.

The effort has succeeded dramatically, particularly in the case of Down Syndrome, the most frequently occurring genetic disorder. Far more women now are able to detect Down Syndrome pregnancies, and far more end them with abortion. Yet even as it becomes easier and more common to prevent children with Down Syndrome from being born, the justification for doing so grows murkier.

Unlike many other genetic anomalies, such as Tay-Sachs and anencephaly, Down Syndrome (also known as Down's Syndrome or Trisomy 21) is not a terminal disorder. Children born with Down Syndrome are not vegetables, nor are their lives demonstrably not worth living. Indeed, advances in science and changes in public perception have combined to make Down Syndrome a relatively mild birth defect: The average child born with Down Syndrome in America today can expect to reside at home, go to school, learn to read, hold a job, and live to the age of fifty-five. He will grow up cognizant of ethics and events, and will be mildly to moderately retarded, with an IQ of between 55 and 70. It is one of the triumphs of modern society that the life of the average person with Down Syndrome has become strikingly normal. Except that, unlike normal people, people with Down Syndrome have been targeted for elimination.

Of 22,000 women who received prenatal diagnosis in one 1990 study in Canada, 88 percent of those who found they were carrying a child with Down Syndrome aborted the fetus. Other studies have put the rate of Down Syndrome abortions at about 90 percent, some even higher.

Last year, British journalist Dominic Lawson published an article in the *London Spectator* about the birth of his daughter, who has Down Syndrome. Lawson, a self-described atheist, expressed outrage at the National Health Service's policy of providing free prenatal tests for, and complimentary abortions of, babies with Down Syndrome. He went on to compare the policy to the Nazi eugenics program. Lawson's article was reprinted in the *Daily Mail,* prompting scores of letters to the editor and counter articles. Partly in response to what Lawson had written, a bill was introduced in the House of Lords that would outlaw abortions conducted solely to prevent the birth of a child with Down Syndrome. (Currently, abortion of "seriously handicapped" children, including those with Down Syndrome, is legal in England through the ninth month.) A national debate has begun.

So far, no such public discussion has broken out in the

United States, where amniocentesis and other genetic tests have been used to target Down Syndrome pregnancies for abortion since at least the late 1960s. In 1959, French geneticist Jerome Lejeune discovered that people with Down Syndrome have an extra chromosome responsible for the disorder. The discovery soon made it possible to detect the presence of Down Syndrome in utero. Grasping the implications of his work, Lejeune grew to be a passionate opponent of abortion and prenatal testing, which he called "biological pornography."

But Lejeune could not stop what he had unwittingly begun. By the summer of 1967, the American Medical Association had passed a resolution endorsing abortion in cases in which "an infant may be born with incapacitating physical deformity or mental deficiency." A year later, the American College of Obstetricians and Gynecologists came out with a similar policy. A number of states, years before *Roe v. Wade,* followed suit with laws allowing abortion for the purpose of eliminating children with mental defects, including Down Syndrome.

During the 1970s, genetic testing of pregnant women became routine, a practice encouraged by groups like Planned Parenthood. Since it is an invasive procedure that entails extracting amniotic fluid with a needle from around the child, amniocentesis (like its alternative, chorionic villous sampling) carries a significant risk of miscarriage, in some places as high as one in 100. As a result, the test generally has been reserved for use by women over the age of thirty-four, who are more willing to weigh the risk against that of having a child with Down Syndrome. (The incidence of Down Syndrome increases with maternal age, from about 1 in 2,000 births at age 20 to 1 in 10 at age 49.) In 1984, however, it was discovered that a noninvasive blood test could be used to calculate the likelihood of bearing a Down Syndrome child. The blood test made it possible to provide screening for Down Syndrome to women of all ages, at no risk to the mother. In 1986, the state of California began requiring physicians to offer the tests to pregnant women. The state's health department now funds much of the screening itself, spending $56 million a year to detect prenatal birth defects.

The rest of the country followed California's lead. Between 1988 and 1993, the number of pregnant women who received blood tests for Down Syndrome doubled, to about 2 million. Almost all the tests were covered by private health insurance or Medicaid. Last year, the American College of Obstetricians and Gynecologists officially recommended Down Syndrome screening for all pregnant women. Although there is no cure or prevention for Down Syndrome—indeed, the only real intervention that can be taken after a positive test result is abortion—prenatal screening is now, in effect, mandatory. Few physicians, regardless of their beliefs on the subject, are willing to risk not offering the test, for fear of being slapped with a "wrongful birth" suit if a handicapped child is born. It has happened, repeatedly.

The rapid growth of prenatal testing has had some undeniably positive effects: A woman who knows she will bear a child with a handicap can plan to deliver in a hospital equipped for risky births. And many couples prefer the opportunity to prepare psychologically for the work of raising a disabled child. By far the most profound effect of prenatal testing, however, has been a staggering increase in the number of abortions.

The trend is clear: more testing invariably leads to more—many more—abortions of Down Syndrome children. "Most women who have children with Down Syndrome did not have the amnio," says Lori Atkins of the National Down Syndrome Society, and there is growing evidence to indicate this is true. A study of data from selected states by the Centers for Disease Control found that the rate of Down Syndrome births to mothers thirty-five or older dropped by about a third between 1983 and 1990. Another study, conducted over a slightly longer period, pegged the decline at 46 percent.

Larry Edmunds, a CDC statistician who is among the country's acknowledged experts on birth-defect trends, cites data from the 1980s suggesting that abortion reduced the number of children with Down Syndrome born to white women over thirty-five in the metropolitan Atlanta area by about 70 percent. Of the 30 percent in that study who did bear children with Down Syndrome, Edmunds explains, "those were mainly women who didn't have the test."

Lewis Holmes, a professor of pediatrics at Harvard Medical School who works at Massachusetts General Hospital, says that in his experience, of women who learn they are carrying a Down Syndrome child, "90 percent will say they want to terminate. If you have all the technology available and educate the women as to what their choices are, that will happen."

Far fewer than 90 percent of women support abortion,

at least in the abstract, so there is some question as to why so many are choosing it when they find they are carrying children with Down Syndrome. A number of studies have attempted to provide an answer. One, conducted by the Canadian Royal Commission on New Reproductive Technologies, found that, because of pressure from hospital staff, one in four pregnant women "felt obliged" to undergo amniocentesis. Of those who tested positive for a birth defect, one in three believed she was "more or less forced" to have an abortion.

Another study, published this summer in the *British Medical Journal,* describes the case of one pregnant woman whose child had tested positive for birth defects. Following her doctor's orders, she reported to the labor ward of her hospital for what the physician had termed an "induction." It dawned on the woman, who was five months pregnant, that the "induction" was in fact to be an abortion. Horrified, she returned home and later bore the child.

Laurie Cowan, a physician at the state of Delaware's public health department, readily admits that abortion has had a dramatic effect on births of children with Down Syndrome. "We are seeing a real drop in the rate of [Down Syndrome] children who are born. We're not seeing a drop in the rate of children who are conceived," she says. But like many in the medical profession, Cowan is wary of how such information might be used. Abortion, she explains, "has been a right that people have had. So I hope that in no way you'll do anything to try to take away that right. I'm just very concerned about that. I just hope in no way your work will undermine that." Anti-abortion forces, she warns, would allow the procedure "only if the mother is raped, only if she's going to die because of this pregnancy. And that's uncomfortable for me because there are certain things that are pretty close to that."

Having a Down Syndrome child is close to being raped? To dying?

Why such eagerness to prevent Down Syndrome children from being born? Undoubtedly, some physicians are motivated by a belief that children with birth defects pollute the gene pool. "There is nothing wrong with eugenics," said Dr. F. Clarke Fraser, founder of the genetics clinic at Montreal Children's Hospital, not long ago in an unusually blunt interview with the *Montreal Gazette*.

Many others, however, simply view abortion and Down Syndrome as parts of an economic equation. Amniocentesis "may cost about $1,000, but a reasonably conservative estimate is that it costs $100,000 for just the first year of a Down Syndrome baby's life," explained Dr. Mark Evans, director of Detroit's Center for Fetal Diagnosis and Therapy. "How many people would I have to test to balance the lifetime cost?" he asked a *New York Times* reporter in what must rank among the creepiest rhetorical questions ever posed. "And then there are economic considerations nobody knows how to factor in, like the number of women who would have to quit their careers to care for these babies."

Actually, Dr. Evans was wrong on at least one count: a number of people have "factored in" the various costs of Down Syndrome. A 1995 study led by Norman Waitzman of the University of Utah sought to calculate the toll that birth defects take on the American economy. The results, published in a CDC report, found that each child born with Down Syndrome will, over a lifetime, cost society about $451,000. The total cost for all children born with the disorder in a given year, the study determined, is $1.8 billion. "Particularly in these times of fiscal squeeze," he concluded, "these costs provide a vivid picture of the value of research and prevention."

Needless to say, Waitzman failed to point out that, in the case of Down Syndrome, there's no way to "prevent" the disorder, only the birth of those afflicted with it. Obscured by euphemisms or not, calculations such as Waitzman's have not escaped the attention of insurance companies, many of which have proved indecorously eager to cover testing for potentially expensive genetic defects, most recently for cystic fibrosis.

Nachum Sicherman of the Columbia Business School, another researcher who has examined the "enormous cost-saving potential of amniocentesis," is the sort of expert insurance companies doubtless will consult as they begin to sort out the growing number of prenatal genetic tests in order to determine which ones they should pay for. Sicherman figures the cost to society over the lifetime of a person with Down Syndrome is at least $1 million—most of which, he points out, "is not going to be paid by parents." Numbers like these—and Sicherman's are larger than most—have led Sicherman to recommend that amniocentesis be made available to all nearly pregnant women, regardless of age. "If you take all costs into account—costs to school districts, to Medicare, Medicaid, Social Security, lost days of work for parents," he explains enthusiastically, "there is nothing more beneficial than amniocentesis, if it is given under the assumption that if Down Syndrome is discovered, there is an abortion following. It's a great cost saving."

Sicherman does more than simply theorize on the subject. "When my wife was pregnant," he recalls, "we went to Lamaze class and I asked the women there if they'd ever heard of amniocentesis." Being a mostly young and lower-income group, he says, none had, and Sicherman did his best to remedy their ignorance. It was, after all, only the right thing to do. "Everybody should tell their patients about amniocentesis," he says.

Sicherman's views may be a bit blunt for the present state of public opinion in America. Not so in the Netherlands, however, where subjecting pregnancy to rigorous economic calculation is considered a civic responsibility. A 1991 report by the Royal Dutch Society of Medicine (titled "Life Terminating Actions with Incompetent Patients, Part I: Severely Handicapped Newborns") studied a series of 2,816 amniocenteses given to pregnant women. The tests resulted in 75 abortions, 57 of which were of " defective fetuses."

"These 2,816 amniocenteses and the chromosome analyses cost approximately $1.5 million," the study said. "This is in the same order of magnitude as the costs for taking care of one patient with Down's Syndrome in a medical institution for a period of 60 years. Seen in the light of a cost-benefit analysis the conclusion is obvious."

From here, it is a short trip to killing handicapped children outright. Why, after all, stop the economizing simply because a child has left the womb? James D. Watson, who won the Nobel Prize for the discovery of DNA, believed that newborns who scored below a certain level on the Apgar test given immediately after birth should be euthanized.

In fact, infants with Down Syndrome are routinely starved to death in Dutch hospitals—a practice that has been resoundingly affirmed by both that country's supreme court and its Council for Children's Protection. Nor are such practices restricted to the Netherlands. A 1975 poll found that 77 percent of American pediatric surgeons favored withholding food and medical treatment from infants with Down Syndrome and leaving them to die. Seven years later, in the well-publicized Baby Doe case, a Bloomington, Indiana, couple asked their doctor to do just that to their child born with Down Syndrome. The infant, who needed only simple surgery to correct a blocked esophagus, died after six days of neglect. In a strikingly similar incident several years later in Montreal, a Down Syndrome child died after eleven days without food or water. "The presence of Down Syndrome," said a local coroner, "was another element [in the decision to kill the child] since mongolism implies a quasi-vegetative life or severely diminished quality of life."

Given these stories and the evidence that an entire population of retarded people may be wiped clean from this country, one would expect organizations that represent the disabled to be up in arms.

One would expect wrong.

"We have a clear position not to take a position on the issue of abortion," says Paul Marchand, head lobbyist at the Arc (formerly known as the Association for Retarded Citizens), one of the country's largest such groups. The National Down Syndrome Congress, in its "Position Statement on Prenatal Testing and Eugenics," is equally explicit: "These positions . . . in no way involve the movement in the debate over whether a woman should have a legal right to abortion."

Disability groups tend to be on edge when it comes to public perceptions of the mentally retarded. (Al Gore learned this the hard way when he referred to Oliver North's political supporters as "the extra-chromosome right wing," drawing roars of protest from Down Syndrome groups.) They are quick to spot even the most subtle forms of discrimination—the Arc actually has an official policy demanding equal access to dental treatment. So it is puzzling that so few groups have seen fit to comment on the growth of state-endorsed eugenics targeted—in the most discriminatory, dehumanizing way imaginable—at their own constituents. It's a little like the NAACP refusing to come out against slavery.

In 1978, the Delaware chapter of the Association for Retarded Citizens did take a position: it passed a resolution demanding that the federal government pay for abortions for poor women who learn they are carrying potential retarded citizens. The resolution prompted the Arc's national organization to convene a task force on the issue. After months of work, the group produced a sixty-page report declaring that, although a majority of its members supported government funding for the abortion of retarded children, a unanimous decision could not be reached. And that, says lobbyist Marchand, was that: "I don't think anything on abortion has crossed my desk in the last ten years." The only comparable issue today, he says, is the debate within the "disability community" over whether it is valid to search for a cure for mental retardation. "It can be a touchy subject," he explains without a hint of irony, because when you seek a cure, "what you're doing de facto is devaluing people with mental retardation."

Not that the Arc spends a lot of time pondering existential questions like these. The group's real concern nowadays, says Marchand, is "the federal role in the future of mental retardation"—that is, getting more money from the government. He rattles off a list of programs his organization is lobbying to maintain and expand: Medicaid, Social Security, disability insurance, job training, special education. "We are extremely occupied with a myriad of federal policy issues that are before us," Marchand says. "Our plate is more than overflowing."

Meanwhile, as the Arc concerned itself with its "myriad of federal policy issues," another issue was being decided on Capitol Hill, one from which the voice of the disability lobby was noticeably absent: partial-birth abortion. The vast majority of Down Syndrome children identified in utero are diagnosed using amniocentesis, which is not even performed until the sixteenth week of pregnancy. The abortions that result are of the grisly variety, some of them performed by the skull-crushing partial-birth technique on infants capable of living outside the womb.

During the debate over the procedure, the Clinton administration cited the record of abortion doctor James McMahon as evidence that a ban on partial-birth abortions would be unacceptably rigid. The pregnant women McMahon had treated, the administration argued, had received abortions to alleviate the sort of "serious health problems" that should be exempted under the ban. And what were these problems? According to data the doctor himself provided to Congress, the single most common "serious fetal defect" McMahon " treated" was Down Syndrome.

It would be unfair to single out organized Down Syndrome groups for their unwillingness to confront the subject of abortion, since the willful blindness runs much deeper. In *Life as We Know It,* his recent book about raising a son with Down Syndrome, Michael Bérubé describes the typical response on an internet discussion group when the subject of prenatal testing and abortion arises: "Every time someone brings up the question on the listserv, he or she is met with dozens of e-mail responses reading 'NO! NO! NOT ON THIS LIST! Please don't have this discussion here! There are plenty of other newsgroups for this debate. This is about children with disabilities.'"

Dr. Bill Cohen of the Down Syndrome Center of Western Pennsylvania, a noted authority on the disorder, has much the same response when asked about his views on abortion. "If someone comes to me and says that they're thinking about terminating the pregnancy, my job is not to convince them not to," he says. "This is not a right-to-life issue. This is a choice issue. This is an information issue. . . . It's hard enough to deal with any of these things without being made to feel on top of it that you've done something wrong."

Yet, it's difficult to shake the feeling that those who abort a child simply because he or she has Down Syndrome have done something wrong. Children with Down Syndrome are not monsters, but uncommonly gentle human beings who can and do lead full lives. And there are alternatives to abortion. "It's not at all difficult" to find homes for kids with Down Syndrome, says Janet Marchese of the Down Syndrome Adoption Exchange in White Plains, New York, one of several agencies of its kind in the United States. Over the past twenty years, Marchese has placed about 3,600 children with Down Syndrome; her waiting list of couples hoping to adopt rarely dips below 100.

What do people who would adopt a Down Syndrome child know that most obstetricians do not? "Having a child with Down Syndrome is not such a big deal—if you have some experience with Down Syndrome you realize that," says Nancy Simpson of Chesapeake Down Syndrome Parent Group in Phoenix, Maryland, whose eight-year-old daughter has Down Syndrome. "It's definitely not as easy as raising a typical child; there are a lot of things that are involved in it. Raising a child with Down Syndrome takes extra patience and extra care and extra time. But you also get back a completely different perspective on the world, and a great deal of love."

Sentiments like these are almost unimaginable to Jeffrey Greenspoon, M.D. Greenspoon is the director of the high-risk obstetric unit at Cedars-Sinai Medical Center in Los Angeles. In the summer of 1995, during the beginning of the debate over partial-birth abortion, Greenspoon sent a letter to Representative Henry Hyde passionately defending the procedure, especially in cases where a child might be born with "problems . . . incompatible with a normal life," such as Down Syndrome.

"A pregnancy that is desired and planned is the foundation for the next generation of productive, healthy Americans," Greenspoon wrote. "The burden of raising one or two abnormal children is realistically unbearable."

Reached at his office, Greenspoon admits that he approves of eugenics—weeding out "babies who don't have much of a viable life." What makes him uncomfortable, he says, is the word "eugenics," which somehow has assumed "bad connotations over time. I think the better terms would be 'genetic counseling' and 'prenatal diagnosis' and 'having a country in which the option to exercise choice in whether to continue or terminate a pregnancy is a right of the people.'" After all, he says, "Sometimes you need to abandon words that have common meanings that connote the wrong ethics or morals."

But only the words have changed.

———

I was in my mid-forties before I realized what an unusual childhood I had. Maybe everyone's that way: you assume your friends were raised exactly the way you were. But in my case, they weren't. No one I know had a father like mine. My father was funnier and more outrageous, more creative and less willing to conform, than anyone I knew, or have known since. My brother and I had the best time growing up. I probably revealed too much in this essay, but every word is true and I laughed out loud as I wrote it.

"DANGEROUS TOYS"

Dadly Virtues, 2015

I've heard people say they never really felt like adults until their parents died. That makes sense, but it's not how I made my final break with childhood. Mine came while walking through Wal-Mart not long after my thirty-fifth birthday. I'd come to buy a trash can but somehow found myself in the sporting goods aisle, standing in front of the largest display of BB guns I'd ever seen. There were Daisy Red Ryders and scoped Beeman target rifles, CO_2-powered pellet pistols, and something called the Gamo Buckmaster Squirrel Terminator. I counted at least a dozen Crosman 760 Pumpmasters, a weapon regarded by every boy in my sixth grade class as the AK-47 of air rifles for its power and durability.

For a full minute I stared. Man, I wish I could get one of those, I thought.

Then it dawned on me: I'm a grown man with a valid driver's license. I can buy as many BB guns as I want.

So I did.

In the end I bought one of each. On my way to the checkout counter, I spotted blowguns for sale. They were four feet long and made of machined aircraft-grade aluminum, each with a quiver of steel knitting needles for darts. "Deadly accurate at ranges of more than 20 yards," the package promised. I bought a couple of them. Then I drove home and gave the entire arsenal to my kids to play with. In my house, we believe in dangerous toys.

It's a faith I inherited. One of my earliest and most vivid memories starts on a dirt road in Southern California early in the Carter presidency. I'm seven, my brother is five. We are lying facedown on the roof of our family's 1976 Ford Country Squire station wagon, a wood-paneled land yacht almost nineteen feet long. My father is in the driver's seat smoking a Pall Mall. "Hold on," he yells through the open window. My brother and I grip the leading edge of the luggage rack, splaying our legs like snipers. My father guns the massive V8 and we shoot forward at high speed over culverts and potholes and rocks. At one especially steep hump in the road we seem to catch air and I look over in time to see my brother in flight, tethered to the vehicle only by his fingertips. His mouth is opened wider than I have ever seen it. He is screaming with happiness.

I've sometimes wondered what car surfing was meant to teach us. My father had a reckless streak but he was kind, and always deliberate. Every activity came with a message about deeper truths. Was he trying to instill in us a proper sense of fatalism, the acknowledgment that there is only so much in life you can control? Or was it a lesson about the importance of risk? "Who dares, wins," he often said, quoting the motto of the Special Air Service. Until you're willing to ride the roof of a speeding station wagon, in other words, you're probably not going to leave your mark on the world.

That's all wise advice, if seldom heard anymore, and I've done my best to pass it on to my own four children. But I suspect there was another motive at work. My father loved dangerous toys because dangerous toys are the most interesting kind. Sure, it's momentarily entertaining to watch a Slinky walk down stairs, but spend an afternoon playing with lawn darts, and you're apt to learn an enduring lesson or two. Dangerous toys are an education. By that measure, my brother and I were the most erudite kids in the neighborhood.

One of the first things we learned was that shopping carts aren't built for speed. We'd liberated one from a nearby supermarket and decided to race it down the hill in front of our house. Since he was younger and less aware of consequences, my brother climbed into the basket and took the first ride. Within ten feet, all four wheels turned sideways and he wound up with a bloody nose and gravel in both palms. After that we stuck to mopeds, scooters and riding our skateboards while holding car bumpers.

Shortly after my sixteenth birthday, my father decided it was time for me to learn to drive a car. He gave me the first lesson himself, in a movie theater parking lot. Then he rented me a car for a month and wished me luck. It was a white Chrysler with an AM radio and a manual transmission. I drove it all over San Diego, leaving clouds of melting clutch at intersections.

After a while it seemed prudent to get a driver's license. There was a written test and a driving exam, but before taking either I had to spend a week at a state-approved driver's education course. It was held in a strip mall, six hours a day, and it was deadly boring. Classes seemed to consist entirely of lectures on speed limits and unintentionally hilarious DUI videos. I drove myself to and from school every day.

By Thursday, this had caught the attention of the kid sitting next to me, a droopy-eyed stoner with a blond butt cut and a pukka shell necklace. During lunch break, he confronted me. "Wait a minute, dude," he said, obviously baffled. "We're in driving class, so we can get a driver's license, to drive. But you drove here. How'd you do that?"

Good question. My father laughed when I told him about it.

My father was famous among our friends for his sense of humor, and for letting us do perilous things with vehicles. But by far the most dangerous thing he ever let us do was root around unsupervised in his library, which was vast and eclectic. He had books on virtually everything interesting and weird, from accounts of cannibalism in Micronesia to transcripts of court-martials from the Boer War. He had an especially large collection of extremist literature he'd picked up while covering the lunacy of San Francisco in the 1960s as a reporter. I'll never forget the day we came across *The Anarchist Cookbook*. It was on a high shelf next to *The Poor Man's James Bond*.

Both books have since been the subject of court cases, and it's easy to see why. Not only do they endorse the violent overthrow of the existing order, but they offer detailed instructions on how to achieve it using common household items. Within days my brother and I had constructed a remarkably effective flamethrower.

From there we moved to ordnance. One day after school we built improvised hand grenades using hydrochloric acid we'd bought for $1.50 a gallon in the pool cleaning section of the hardware store. Pour half a pint into a glass bottle, add some bits of aluminum foil, cap tightly, and get away fast. The things went off like a 12-gauge, leaving a satisfying cloud of chlorine gas. We spent many happy hours lobbing them onto the golf course near our house.

There may have been such as thing as travel soccer when I was a kid, but I never heard of it. Nor did we ever seem to have much homework. What we did have was lots of free time, and we spent most of it in martial pursuits. We made nunchakus out of broom handles and throwing stars from circular saw blades. We staged elaborate bottle rocket wars and had pellet gun skirmishes in the backyard. (In a misguided nod to safety, my brother insisted we wear glass diving masks for eye protection.) We constructed a pair of enormous slingshots from rubber surgical tubing and fired water balloons at each other. We played mumblety-peg with kitchen knives and screwdrivers.

Sometimes, when we were feeling ambitious, we took the trolley to Tijuana. After decades of being invaded by Marines on leave from Camp Pendleton, downtown Tijuana was an open-air vice mall, though relatively safe as long as you didn't argue with anybody. In 1981, there was nothing evil you couldn't find there. For the older kids, the lure was tequila and hookers, and the countless unregulated pharmacies that sold codeine-based cough syrup and over-the-counter Percocet. For us, it was all about the switchblades and fireworks, especially the fireworks.

Tijuana firecrackers were the size of Twinkies, made from rolled newspaper and sulfurous gunpowder and painted red, like sticks of dynamite from a Roadrunner cartoon. You could buy them by the pound in plastic grocery bags. Every bag identified them as M-80s, but we knew better. Quality control was an abstract concept in pre-NAFTA Mexico, so each firecracker promised an exciting new surprise. Some sputtered harmlessly, while others left craters in the lawn. Some did both, posing as duds until you walked over to them, at which point they exploded, leaving you deaf for the day.

One afternoon I headed to a friend's house to field-test a new batch of explosives. He lived more than mile away, mostly uphill, so instead of riding my bike I decided to take the go-kart my brother and I had gotten for Christmas. I don't know where my father bought it, but the machine looked homemade, with a plumbing pipe frame, lawn mower engine, and no muffler. It rode just a few inches off the pavement. You could hear it three streets over.

I made it out of our neighborhood to the main intersection in town, where I waited in traffic for the stoplight to change. As I idled there thinking about firecrackers, I noticed people in the cars around me staring down at the go-kart. They looked slightly alarmed, but nobody said anything. The light changed and I drove off with my sack of M80s. Later that day I drove home. It was a different country then.

By the time my own children were born, there were no more go-karts on city streets. America's moms were firmly in charge, and that meant safety was a virtue for its own sake, a concept that had never occurred to me growing up. There wasn't much I could do about it. You might not like a cultural consensus but bucking it is fruitless, if not illegal. At the very least it exposes you as a crank.

So I made do with low-grade subversion. My father helped, by regularly giving the kids shotguns and Masai war spears for Christmas. I did my part by letting them steer the car while sitting on my lap, which of course they loved. That continued until I bought a new car and discovered that its air bags could be fatal to small children. Pretty ironic, I huffed to my mechanic that a device designed to protect us might wind up killing my kids. He looked at me blankly, and flat-out refused when I asked him to disconnect them. "Air bags are mandatory," he said. "It's the law." There's no fighting the Mommy State.

Except possibly with potato cannons. That was my hope when I bought them, anyway. A potato cannon is a length of plastic drain pipe, capped on one end, with a barbecue ignitor set in the back as a trigger. Filled with a flammable aerosol like hairspray or underarm deodorant, it becomes the homeowner's RPG. It will fire a baked potato the span of a football field and through a Sheetrock wall. It also shoots limes and peaches and apples and chunks of ice. I live in a house with three daughters, so it was only a matter of time before we loaded the thing with Barbie dolls.

It happened after lunch in late August one year, on one of those sweltering days that make you want to do something wrong. My son suggested firing a Barbie out of the cannon, which struck me as inspired. So, over his sisters' objections, we did.

The result was an epiphany. I wasn't there when scientists mixed chocolate with peanut butter to produce the world's first Reese's cup, but the moment had that same feeling of harmonic convergence. The doll left the muzzle with its hair on fire and continued to blaze like a plastic meteor all the way over the house onto the front lawn. Even my daughters were in awe.

Before long there was a crowd of neighborhood kids in our yard waiting for me to do it again. I took the opportunity to tell them the following story, which by the way was pretty much true:

A couple of years ago in Texas, I said, a couple of boys loaded a potato cannon with a live bullfrog. Everything went fine until one of the boys decided to peer down the muzzle. You can guess what happened next. The gun went off. He wound up blind. Doctors are still picking pieces of frog out of his face.

The kids listened slack-jawed to the tale, which was both a reminder to be cautious around guns, and a warning against cruelty to animals. Parable delivered, I prepared to blast another Barbie over the roof. "Ready! Aim! Fire!" the kids chanted. I hit the igniter. Nothing happened. I hit it again. Silence.

That's when I did something I still regret, and my kids still talk about. I unscrewed the back of the gun, stuck my face close to the combustion chamber, and, unaccountably, pressed the igniter.

The fireball that emerged vaporized most of the hair above my shoulders, including my eyelashes, eyebrows, and everything else back to the top of my head. I looked freakish, like a clown, or Liza Minnelli's fourth husband. My wife was horrified—and, worse, vindicated. Consider the upside, I said. At least the kids learned something.

———

The question is not: Have you ever been taken for money by a scam artist junkie posing as a stranded diplomat? The question is: Will you admit that you have? In my case, yes, I will. Here's my confession.

"DEREK RICHARDSON, WHERE ARE YOU?"

Weekly Standard, February 19, 1996

Peple don't usually rap on my car window at red lights, so I was a little startled when, on my way to work a few months ago, I turned to find a man peering in at me and mouthing what seemed to be an urgent message. "My car got towed," he said once I'd rolled down the window. "Can you help me?" The light was changing and the man was reasonably well dressed, so I told him to get in. It didn't take long to discover that he was hoping to borrow money.

We drove on and my new friend explained his recent travails, but I wasn't really listening. My thoughts had turned back four years, to the last time a " stranded motorist" hit me up for a short-term loan. My editor and I had pulled into a service station in a seedy part of northeast Washington, D.C., for a fill-up.

As I walked back to the car after paying for the gas, a man in his thirties in a ratty-looking parka sidled up to me. "Can I talk to you for a second?" he asked. It turned out his car, a rusting heap parked across the street, had just blown a distributor valve. Or a Johnson ring. Or a fribulator gasket. Or some other esoteric but absolutely vital piece of engine equipment. A replacement would be cheap and easy to get, but unfortunately—and this was the worst part, he said—he had left all his credit cards at home that day. All he needed was seven dollars to get his car going again, and could I lend it to him? He'd mail me a check as soon as he got back to his house. He promised.

I stepped back to take a look at the man. He looked dirty and shaky and short of teeth. And he talked too fast, managing to come off as demented and sly at the same time. I should have walked away then. His story didn't make sense. No civilized nation would have issued this guy a driver's license, much less let him drive. But I didn't walk away. Instead, I forked over the money, along with my address, written on the back of a parking stub. I wanted to believe I had found Washington's one honest beggar.

"Think you'll ever see your seven dollars again?" my editor asked when I got back into the car. He spoke with a mixture of pity and fascination, in the tone one reserves for the truly stupid. "No question," I said. "I'm sure he's good for it."

To nobody's surprise, he wasn't.

The con artist at the gas station and the fellow I had just picked up seemed to have little in common. For one thing, this guy didn't look like a drug addict. More telling, he appeared to have a legitimate job. His name, he said, was Derek Richardson, and he worked as a teacher at the "Foreign Service School in Bonn, Germany." He had been in Washington on vacation for less than twenty-four hours when his car, which contained his wallet and passport, had been carted away by overzealous parking police. "I should have known it would happen," he said. "I went to school here. At Georgetown."

Pretty convincing stuff. So I lent him forty-eight dollars to get his car out of hock. "Please send back the money," I said before dropping him off near the DMV. "You'll wreck my faith in this kind of thing if you don't." He looked surprised I'd even question him. "No doubt, man. And I really appreciate it."

Needless to say, that was the last I heard from Derek Richardson. After a few weeks of waiting for the check, I decided to track him down. I called the State Department personnel office, scanned the federal employees' directory, harassed the lady at the registrar's office at Georgetown. Not a trace of Derek Richardson. Finally, I called the American embassy in Bonn. The woman I spoke to seemed confused, both by the name Derek Richardson and by the institution he had claimed to work for. "The Foreign Service School?" she asked, the familiar pity creeping into her voice. "There's no such thing."

Normally I would have given up, but by this point I was determined to catch up with Derek Richardson. So I ran his name through Nexis, in the hope he might have cheated somebody else in a newsworthy way. He hadn't, but his name certainly had been a lot of places. Derek Richardson, it turned out, was a fireman in Louisville, an astrophysicist in Toronto, an employee of a dog-food company in London, a high school debate champion in Atlanta, the chairman of the National Farmers' Union in England, and a referee in the NBA. Several years ago, he was a murder victim in New Orleans.

Derek Richardson seemed to be everywhere. Except where he really was, cadging money from dummies like me at red lights. That was the one identity he didn't seem to have. I guess they never do.

———

Who was this ersatz "Derek Richardson" I met at my car window? Amazingly, I found out in the end. Lesson: If you wait long enough, every mystery is solved.

"DEREK RICHARDSON RETURNS"

Weekly Standard, August 4, 1997

E ven at a downtown intersection at 8:45 in the morning, I recognized the man the moment he rapped on my car window. He was wearing a tweed sport coat with leather patches on the elbows and a rep stripe tie. He had a bulky ring of keys in his hand, and he looked frustrated and impatient, like a late-for-work lawyer. "Can you help me?" he asked. "My car's been towed." I couldn't suppress a grin. "Love to," I said. "Get in."

I must have come off as a bit too enthusiastic, because he hesitated for a second before opening the door. But I couldn't control myself. I'd been waiting a year and a half for this moment, ever since the first time this guy approached me at a red light and asked for money. At the time, he called himself Derek Richardson. He said he had been on vacation in Washington for only a few hours when his car was carted off by the city's overzealous parking police. He needed forty-eight dollars to get it back, he said, and could I help him? He promised to repay the money the second he got back to his job at the "Foreign Service School in Bonn, Germany."

It was a pretty good story. I fell for it, at least. Lots of other people must have, too, because eighteen months later, the guy hadn't changed a single word. He was still Derek Richardson, still just in from Bonn. And, of course, he still needed forty-eight dollars. He was as personable as ever. "Where do you work?" he asked as we inched along through rush-hour traffic in search of a cash machine. I told him, and he nodded knowingly. "Doesn't Mort Kondracke work at the *Standard*?" Sure does, I said. Great guy, too.

By the time I spotted a car of uniformed Secret Service agents parked a block from my office, Derek and I were chatting like old friends. "People are so cold-hearted," he said. "You know, you're the first person . . ." He stopped in midsentence when he saw the squad car. "What are we doing here?" he asked as we pulled up to the curb. "Oh," I said, "there's a great cash machine in this building," pointing to the headquarters of the American Association of University Women. "We can get tons of money out of it." "Cool," he said.

Within moments I was out of the car and making a scene. "This guy stole money from me," I yelled as passersby looked on confused. The Secret Service agents scrambled over, and the four of us spent the next half an hour on the sidewalk waiting for the District police to arrive.

I found out pretty fast that the man's name was not Derek Richardson. According to the driver's license he produced, he was Jeffrey A. Cohen, a thirty-six-year-old resident of Springfield, Virginia. Nor, it became clear the longer I looked at him, was he a late-for-work lawyer. Squinting in the sunlight, chain-smoking Marlboros and shaking, Cohen looked a lot like a junkie.

A local cop finally showed up, and I explained what had happened. The cop snorted dismissively. "There's nothing criminal here," he said. "You gave him the money. It doesn't matter whether he said he was Bill Clinton or Uncle Sam. You gave it to him. He didn't do anything fraudulent. This is not a police matter." Cohen looked at me and smiled. Then he walked away.

It wasn't the first time he'd gotten off lightly. Cohen, according to court records I found later, has been convicted of all sorts of crimes over the past ten years, including possession of narcotics, theft, and at least three counts of forgery. He's served some time, but not much. Looking at his record, I became even more determined to get my money back. Before he left, Cohen had given the police his home phone number. I wrote it down on my hand as he spoke. One afternoon, I dialed it. His father, a retired Foreign Service officer, answered the phone. "I don't know anything about it," he said when I told him about Derek Richardson. "It comes as kind of a shock."

Actually, it was obvious the news didn't come as a shock at all, but as another sad reminder of what had become of his son. "We don't see him very often," Cohen's father said wearily. "The only thing I can do is wait till he gets in touch with me and ask him to call you back. Maybe you can get some solid answers out of him."

I didn't have high hopes. But about a week later, I got a message from Cohen on my answering machine. "Hello, Tucker," he said, sounding not at all like a drug-addicted con man, "this is Jeffrey Cohen. I don't have your address to send the money to. I'm calling from a pay phone. I'll try you back later."

He didn't. That was more than three months ago, and I'm still waiting for the call. I'm not discouraged, though. Somehow I know I'll see Jeffrey A. Cohen again. Washington, it turns out, really is a small town.

———————

I wrote this next piece for the long-defunct Talk *magazine, which turned out to be the last serious attempt in this country to create a general-interest monthly. The term "general interest" doesn't even make sense anymore; Americans no longer have enough in common with each other to support any mass-media product. In a divided country, everything is narrowcasting. But in the late 1990s, we didn't know that yet. Tina Brown was the world's most famous magazine editor. She teamed up with, of all people, Harvey Weinstein to create* Talk, *which was supposed to be not simply a magazine, but also a movie company and publishing house. Somehow. In any case, I was one of* Talk's *main political writers. In the spring and summer of 1999, Tina sent me out to profile Texas governor George W. Bush as he prepared to run for president. I spent weeks sitting at the bar in the Driscoll Hotel in Austin on expense account, drinking the local Shiner Bock beer and talking to Bush and his advisers. By the time I finished, I still wasn't sure exactly what I thought of Bush. I'm still not sure, more than twenty years later. Bush is witty as hell, and not nearly as slow as his enemies claim. But still. There's something about him. Complicated guy. This piece comes as close as I ever did to capturing what he's like.*

"DEVIL MAY CARE"

Talk magazine, September 1999

George W. Bush has raised more than $3 million in the past twenty-four hours, and it shows. It's lunchtime on the last day of June, and Bush is riding in the back of a campaign van on his way from the Sacramento airport to a fund-raiser downtown. He looks tired. He holds up a right hand. "Look at that," he says. His palm and knuckles are red and swollen from shaking a thousand hands at five events in four cities. Bush is only about halfway through his first campaign swing across California. There are untold hands left to shake, crowds of donors to pose with in endless mug-a-minute photo opportunities. "Smiling in line for an hour before giving a speech," Bush sighs as he describes how he has spent much of his day. It's enough to wear a man down.

But it has worked. At a press conference two hours ago in Los Angeles, Bush announced that his campaign had raised

147

$36 million so far, a record in American politics. The reporters in the room gasped in surprise when he said it. Bush chuckles at the memory. "The press should have been able to figure it out," he says. "They're not paying much attention. We raised $800,000 in Fort Myers." Bush pauses for a moment, then breaks into a perverse grin. He's had an amusing thought. "What happens if I don't win the nomination."

It's just a joke, of course. Few people, least of all Bush himself, think there's much chance he'll lose it. The national press treats him as though he already has it won. Reporters and camera crews swarm him at every event. Within seconds of crossing the rope line, he is sucked to the center of a mass of straining bodies and becomes invisible, a bobbing head beneath a canopy of boom mikes. It's a level of attention most politicians crave but would have to be indicted to receive. George W. Bush wants you to know he could take it or leave it.

Bush has spent the last day telling audiences that "prosperity must have a purpose," because "prosperity alone is simple materialism." It's unusual to hear a Republican candidate question the intrinsic virtue of capitalism. Bush does it constantly. Over the past several months I've heard him denounce wealth for wealth's sake many times. I've heard him say it over lunch, I've heard him say it while sitting in his living room, riding with him in cars, flying with him in airplanes, talking to him on the phone, interviewing him in his office, and listening to him give speeches in various towns in Texas. Still, I never thought I'd hear him say it at a fund-raising dinner in Southern California. Yet there he was, delivering his mini-sermon to three separate ballrooms of affluent donors, many of whom presumably believe that prosperity is the purpose. No one clapped.

No wonder. What do rich businessmen say when the man they've just given money to tells them that getting rich isn't a noble pursuit? Bush doesn't even wait for me to finish the question. "I don't care. I really don't care. Does anyone ever say 'Fuck you'? I don't care if they do," he barks. "People do have a responsibility to give back, affluent people especially. And that's what I tell them."

You get the sense that if Bush had chosen his own campaign slogan he would have printed bumper stickers that read GEORGE W. BUSH: SO SECURE, HE DOESN'T CARE WHAT YOU THINK OF HIM. As it is, he makes the point as often and as explicitly as he can. Bush's wardrobe, for example, is so inexpensive and fashion-resistant that it can only be understood as a statement of independence. (Though Bush can afford to shop anywhere, he often looks as if he has just returned from an afternoon of shoplifting at Sears.) His stump speeches promise a presidency that will ignore the whims of the people who elect him. "I will not use my office as a mirror to reflect public opinion," he pledges proudly.

Above all, Bush wants to let voters know that he's not desperate for their approval—that unlike Bill Clinton he doesn't have a compelling psychological need to be elected. Politics, Bush often says, is a career he stumbled into. He could stumble out anytime and live the rest of his life content, fishing and basking in the affection of his family. That is, after all, what he says he always planned to do anyway. "I never dreamed about being president of the United States," he says. "It was really never part of my deal." The thought, he claims, only occurred to him about a year ago, "when I started feeling really comfortable in my soul." In the end, Bush explains, "I am, I guess, comfortable enough with myself to know that I may succeed, I may fail, that's okay either way. I look forward to either opportunity."

New Age readers will recognize Bush's explanation as a variation on Deepak Chopra's Law of Detachment, the idea that the less one feels the need to achieve a goal, the more likely one is to achieve it. It's hard to know how seriously to take this. Has there ever been a politician who didn't yearn to be loved by strangers? And why would a presidential candidate "look forward" to the humiliating "opportunity" of defeat? No sane person gives up two years of his life and risks his reputation and his family's comfort and safety for a job he doesn't really care if he gets. Certainly Bush, who is wildly competitive about nearly everything, doesn't seem as if he would. Yet that's his story. He has stuck to it so far.

One thing that Bush seems genuinely not to care about is party affiliation. Bush rarely attacks Democrats in speeches. In Texas he has spent much of his time in politics trying to woo them. Democrats work for him, vote for him, and carry water for his legislation. Mark McKinnon, the media consultant who will oversee his advertising in the 2000 election, once worked for Ann Richards, Bush's opponent in the 1994 governor's race. McKinnon is among Bush's closest advisers, but he makes no effort to look like a Republican. His office is stuffed with Democratic campaign memorabilia. A framed WIN WITH JOHNSON banner hangs over his desk. Signed photographs of prominent Democrats fill an entire bookshelf and most of another wall. McKinnon himself is a former songwriter for Kris Kristofferson. He is happy to discuss his long-standing friendships with Clinton advisers James Carville and Paul Begala.

A few years ago McKinnon decided to retire from politics. He bought part of a hip Austin nightclub and vowed to spend more time with his family. Then he met Bush. Now he is traveling the country shooting footage for Republican campaign ads. (For a documentary effect, McKinnon sometimes uses a Honeywell Filmatic, a dented forty-year-old 8mm home movie camera that belonged to his grandmother.)

McKinnon never became a conservative, but he did fall for Bush. "When I met him," McKinnon recalls, "I was like a married guy who sees an attractive woman at a party and thinks, 'Shit, I've got to stay away from her.' I didn't want to like him. But I couldn't help it." McKinnon picks up one of the dozens of ceramic lizards that sit in a row on his desk, fiddling with it as he searches for superlatives to describe the effect meeting Bush had on him. "I was completely disarmed," he says. "Immediately. He was a completely different person than I'd been led to believe by Democratic propaganda. One of the things that struck me was that he is incredibly confident about who he is. He is incredibly independent of ideological interests, of party interests."

It may have been an independence born of necessity. When Bush first took office in 1995, the Texas statehouse was dom-

inated by Democrats, most notably Lieutenant Governor Bob
Bullock, a fixture in state politics. Governors are weak by design under Texas's constitution, and at the time Bullock was
the most powerful politician in the state. (Though he was never
elected to the office, Bullock was often addressed as "Governor.") A reformed alcoholic and manic-depressive chain smoker
famous for, among other things, getting drunk and firing handguns indoors, Bullock was widely regarded as tough and crafty
and no one to fool with. By the time he died this June he had
become one of Bush's closest political allies.

Soon after Bush was elected, he began inviting Bullock to
breakfast every week and soliciting his advice on politics. The
two worked out compromises on legislation, and when it passed,
Bush was careful to give the lieutenant governor at least half the
credit. At a breakfast meeting during the 1997 legislative session, Bullock told Bush he planned to back a bill Bush opposed.
"I'm sorry, Governor," Bullock said, "but I'm going to have to
fuck you on this one." In front of staff, Bush stood up, grabbed
Bullock by the shoulders, pulled him forward, and kissed him.
"If you're going to fuck me," Bush said, "you'll have to kiss me
first."

Bullock was hooked. The following year Bush ran for reelection against state land commissioner Garry Mauro. Bullock
was godfather to Mauro's daughter but he endorsed Bush anyway. This summer, as he lay dying, Bullock summoned Mark
McKinnon to his house for a final conversation. The two talked
about Bush's performance during his first campaign trip out
of state. "He said, 'He's going to make it and he's going to be

a great president,'" recalls McKinnon, who once worked for Bullock. "Those are the last words I ever had with him."

It's clear that many of those around Bush wind up mesmerized by him. From a distance it's not obvious why. Bush's appeal doesn't come across readily on television, or even from a hundred yards away. He doesn't have the cheery backslapping style of a conventionally charming politician. He's not a flatterer. He doesn't compulsively throw his arms around strangers and claim to feel their pain or read their books or deeply appreciate what they have to say. When he meets someone, Bush stands two paces back and stares. His eyes get beady. He doesn't seem eager, or smile right away. When he talks it's sometimes in grunts and usually out of the side of his mouth. The effect is somewhere between the prelude to a bar fight—What'd you say?— and the way a close friend looks at you before telling you a secret, at once intimate and faintly menacing. It's weirdly compelling.

On the way to a speech outside Austin one day, Bush wades through a sea of well-wishers standing in front of the roped-off podium. People thrust programs in his face, hoping for an autograph. Parents push their children forward to see the man they believe will be president. Bush meets and greets and shakes hands till his eyes fix on a sullen-looking man of about twenty-five with a wispy goatee and a biker T-shirt. The man has a beer in his hand and is hanging back, as if he wandered into the event by accident and is now looking for a way to leave. Before he can, Bush advances, then stops and takes hold of one of his arms, which are pasty white and covered from shoulder to wrist with tattoos. "Where'd you get 'em done?" Bush asks, sounding genuinely impressed by the quality of the snakes, flames, and death's-heads. "Here and there," the man mumbles. Bush nods. "Good," he says. For a moment the man looks confused—is the governor being serious?—then relaxes and smiles. He has been disarmed.

Bush's brand of forthright tough-guy populism can be appealing, and it has played well in Texas. Yet occasionally there are flashes of meanness visible beneath it. While driving back from the speech later that day, Bush mentions Karla Faye Tucker, a double murderer who was executed in Texas last year. In the weeks before the execution, Bush says, Bianca Jagger and a number of other protesters came to Austin to demand clemency for Tucker. "Did you meet with any of them?" I ask.

Bush whips around and stares at me. "No, I didn't meet with any of them," he snaps, as though I've just asked the dumbest, most offensive question ever posed. "I didn't meet with Larry King either when he came down for it. I watched his interview with [Tucker], though. He asked her real difficult questions, like 'What would you say to Governor Bush?'"

"What was her answer?" I wonder.

"Please," Bush whimpers, his lips pursed in mock desperation, "don't kill me."

I must look shocked—ridiculing the pleas of a condemned prisoner who has since been executed seems odd and cruel, even for someone as militantly anticrime as Bush—because he immediately stops smirking. "It's tough stuff," Bush says, suddenly somber, "but my job is to enforce the law." As it turns out, the Larry King–Karla Faye Tucker exchange Bush recounted never took place, at least not on television. During her interview with King, however, Tucker did imply that Bush was succumbing to election-year pressure from pro-death-penalty voters. Apparently Bush never forgot it. He has a long memory for slights.

Which is part of the problem with Bush's presentation of himself as a man so "comfortable in my soul" that he hardly cares whether he wins or loses. Anyone who has reached the Zen-master level of self-acceptance he describes would be unaffected by ordinary criticism. It's still pretty easy to get a rise out of Bush.

One afternoon this spring during a flight back to Austin, Bush's campaign plane navigates along the fringes of a thunderstorm. The little turboprop bucks and shudders, but Bush doesn't seem to notice. Leaning back in his seat, he digs into a bowl of popcorn with one hand and picks at a wad of gum on the sole of his cowboy boot with the other. He's talking about politics and telling stories. He's in an exuberant mood. It seems as good a time as any to ask about the naked picture.

For close to a year a rumor has circulated that the Gore campaign has a photograph of Bush dancing nude on a bar top. So far no one had produced the picture; chances are it doesn't exist. But it has become a metaphor for the sort of questions Bush has to contend with as a candidate and I can't resist bringing it up.

"Before I leave town," I say, "I'd like to get one of those pictures of you dancing. Where can I find one?" Bush stops grinning. His eyes narrow. He puts down the popcorn and thrusts his face toward mine. "People are spreading this garbage," he says angrily. "They think it's like a high school election, where if you beat up your opponent enough you can win. They've lost their fucking minds."

"Who is 'they'? Who's spreading these stories?"

Bush glances around, then lowers his voice to people-are-listening level. "Everyone who's running for president," he whispers.

Bush's staff gets uncomfortable when he talks like this. Though what he has said is true—the other campaigns *are* spreading rumors about him—he runs the risk of sounding like Nixon by saying it out loud. When Bush and I talk about abortion, I ask whether the number of abortions has gone up or down since he's been governor. "I don't know," he shrugs, sounding as though he genuinely doesn't. "Probably down. Not because of anything we've done, though. We haven't passed any laws."

Bush has been under pressure to establish his pro-life bona fides since he first indicated he might run for president, and it seems remarkable that he'd pass up a chance to at least pretend he has reduced the state's abortion rate. Karen Hughes, Bush's communications director, apparently thinks it's remarkable, too. She immediately tries to clarify the record. Hughes, a strikingly tall, fortyish former Dallas television reporter, travels everywhere with Bush and handles him with attentive, motherly concern. She is one of the few people in his entourage who don't hesitate to interrupt him in midsentence. "We've doubled the number of adoptions in Texas," Hughes interjects, looking directly at Bush. "You've done a lot to cut abortions." "That's right," agrees David Sibley, a state senator from Waco and a friend of Bush's who was also on the plane. "The crisis pregnancy centers." Bush gives a pained, don't-spin-*me* look. "We don't fund crisis pregnancy centers," he says crisply.

It's not every day you hear a politician go out of his way to explain that he's not responsible for progress. You get the feeling Bush does it not out of modesty but simply for the pleasure of being blunt. Bush enjoys saying what he thinks, and seems liable to at any moment. No presidential candidate can afford to be too candid—"He used to say 'fuck' a lot more 'efore all this started," says one of his advisers—but after five years as governor, Bush still has the capacity to surprise.

Like when he cries. During a conversation abut a particularly touching letter he once received from his father, Bush's eyes suddenly fill up with tears. It seems remarkable that a man as gruff as Bush would allow himself to get choked up in public. But he doesn't turn away or even seem embarrassed.

Bush believes that his connection to his softer emotional side is part of the key to political success. He became further convinced of this after reading a profile of Al Gore by Louis Menand that ran in *The New Yorker* last year. Bush finished the piece convinced that Gore lacks the warmth and personal appeal necessary to win a presidential race. At one point Gore waxes enthusiastic to Menand about the French philosopher Maurice Merleau-Ponty's *Phenomenology of Perception*, a work,

Gore explains, that he found useful "in cultivating a capacity for a more refined introspection that gave me better questions that ultimately led to a renewed determination to become involved with the effort to make things better." As Menand points out, "It's a little hard to imagine having this conversation with George W. Bush."

And it is. Toward the end of one interview with Bush I decide to test the Larry King Theory—that the dumbest questions are the most evocative—and ask Bush who his heroes are. Expecting the stock Albert Schweitzer–Aristotle–Mother Teresa phoniness, I am surprised when Bush can't seem to come up with an answer. After thinking for an uncomfortably long moment, he names only one: retired baseball player Nolan Ryan. (In the airport later, I notice that Ryan, a close friend of Bush's, happens to be on the cover of that month's *Texas Monthly*.) When I ask Bush to name something he isn't good at, there is no hesitation at all. "Sitting down and reading a five-hundred-page book on public policy or philosophy or something," he says.

Bush isn't ashamed to admit he's not a detail man. Sometimes he brags about it. "I'm not interested in process," he says, almost shouting for emphasis as he speaks. "I want the results. If the process doesn't yield the right results, change the process." As governor, Bush became famous for cutting meetings short, refusing to read memos longer than two pages, and making unusually quick decisions based on instinct and a few simple principles. To this day he sometimes hires high-level staff members the day he meets them. He married his wife about three months after their first date.

His friends make the case that Bush's management style is streamlined and effective rather than shallow and hasty. In private Bush argues that mastery of the specifics is fundamentally irrelevant to his fitness for the White House. It's the themes that count. (Or, as Tony Garza, the Texas state railroad commissioner and a close Bush ally, puts it, "We don't elect mechanics, we elect drivers.") "Nobody needs to tell me what I believe," Bush tells supporters. "But I do need somebody to tell me where Kosovo is. I know how to ask."

Bush may not have sophisticated policy positions, but he's fairly straightforward about the ones he does have. At a lunch in early May at the governor's mansion, Bush addressed a group of about thirty mostly middle-aged business owners from around the country. As the visitors ate, Bush described his achievements as governor, including his campaign to convince Texas teenagers to "abstain from sex until you find the partner you want to marry." Bush was on the verge of another sentence when two women at the back of the room began to snort dismissively. "Abstinence?" heckled one. "Good luck!"

Both women were fiftyish, attractive, and expensively dressed. Both had flown in from out of town that morning on a late-model Learjet. Bush's fund-raising efforts require the support of affluent Republican women like these, few of whom are naturally sympathetic to his views on social issues. Responding to them can be tricky. Promoting abstinence is a relatively small part of Bush's agenda. Wooing donors is vital. Bush could have diluted his position or at least mumbled something about how, while he happens to support the concept of abstinence, he recognizes that choices about how to express human sexuality raise deeply personal issues over which thoughtful people often disagree. He didn't. "Abstinence works," he said. "But it can't work if we don't try it."

The women looked unconvinced. After he finished speaking, Bush walked over to their table and asked them why they seemed skeptical. "Well," replied one, "were *you* a virgin when you got married?" Bush paused for a moment. "No," he answered.

Bush might have come out of the exchange looking like a hypocrite. The women saw it differently. As their jet taxied down the runway of Austin's private airport an hour later, they chatted enthusiastically about Bush's directness, his honesty, the depth of his convictions. "He's so unlike Clinton," said one.

The Bush campaign welcomes sentiments like these, though only rarely does Bush compare himself to Clinton, or even mention the president by name. On the subject of infidelity, however, Bush considers it worthwhile to make clear distinctions. Sometimes at night, Bush says, he and his wife joke about some of the wild stories that have circulated about him. "I tell her all the rumors, of course. Except the womanizing stuff. Everyone knows, should know, that I have been faithful to my wife for the past twenty-one years." Bush proceeds, without being asked, to assure me that he has never committed adultery—not once, not ever, not since the day "I put my hand on the Bible and said 'till death do us part.'"

One of two things is going on here. Either Bush is lying, which would make him the most reckless major-party candidate ever to run for president. (Even Clinton was careful never to categorically deny having cheated on his wife.) Or he's telling the truth. His staff of course, is betting on the latter.

"That's a bedrock issue," says one of his closest advisers. "If it's a lie, he'll get what he deserves."

⸎

The fund-raiser in Sacramento has ended, and Bush has moved on to the next event, an appearance in a nearby park with Oakland Raiders wide receiver Tim Brown. Before he delivers his remarks, Bush throws a football for the kids attending the day camp Brown sponsors. Bush has a pretty good arm, except all of his passes appear to be aimed at the gaggle of reporters watching him from the sidelines. A Fox News correspondent looks up just in time to save his pearly caps from a particularly clean spiral. Bush laughs and cocks his arm again. A newspaper reporter turns out to have slower reflexes. The ball hits him square in the chest, almost knocking him down. Bush throws another, even harder. This one beans a cameraman.

It's clear that Bush is doing this on purpose, but for some reason no one in the press pool seems offended, perhaps because Bush is obviously having such a good time. Almost all politicians claim to like retail campaigning, but most of them look pained when they actually do it. Bush is trotting around the grass with a demented look on his face. He's either a fantastic actor or he's enjoying himself.

It's hard to believe that anyone could enjoy himself while running for president, but with Bush you never know. About two months before Bush's campaign started in earnest, I decided to visit his church, Tarrytown United Methodist in Austin. Bush wasn't there when I arrived, and I almost didn't see him come in right around the time the service started. Bush entered alone, walked with head down up a side aisle, and sat in an empty pew by himself. No one gawked or even seemed to notice him. Nor did Bush glance around the room or make eye contact with strangers the way politicians compulsively do. He just sat there, listened to the sermon, and sang hymns.

He spotted me on the way out. "Hey, man," he said. "Want a ride?" It dawned on me later that Bush never asked where I was going, or why I might need help getting there, or even what I had been doing in his church. But at the time it all seemed perfectly natural. Sure, I said, and we walked outside. Bush greeted a few people he seemed to know—three, by my count—then ambled to the car, and we left. Bush sat in front with the driver, chatting all the way to the governor's mansion. We entered the gates, the driver left, and suddenly there was no one around. Bush's daughters had arrived home from a school prom at 3 a.m. the night before—"sober, I might add," Bush said—and had since gone shopping with their mother. There were no aides or servants or bodyguards in sight. It was almost totally quiet.

The front door of the mansion was unlocked, and Bush left it open as he headed into the kitchen to root around for a Diet Coke. He was talking about how his life was about to change forever, about how he'd never be anonymous again once he had run for president. I had heard Bush say this before, but this time it struck me as real, and kind of sad.

He didn't seem sad about it, though. "I view my life as a series of interesting experiences," Bush said, grinning again. I think he meant it. Suddenly it seemed possible that George W. Bush really could be the one candidate who doesn't need to be president.

————

For decades, the Palm on 19th Street downtown was considered the best restaurant in Washington. Given the city's dining options at the time, that's a little like being described as the sexiest tax lawyer in Century City, or the finest caterer in Ouagadougou. Of course, being Washington, food was never really the point of the Palm. The point was the other people who ate there. At the center of that constellation was the maître d', Tommy Jacomo. Tommy's gone now, along with the bipartisan lunch culture that sustained him. But what a guy. Twenty years ago, he was famous enough that the New York Times asked me to write about him. Unfortunately I had no idea that Tommy had never bothered to tell his children about his cocaine arrest. They learned about it in my story. Tommy was humiliated, and extremely angry at me. Thankfully, with the help of intermediaries, we patched it up before he died. I spent many happy afternoons eating crab cakes in the main dining room and listening to him tell sex jokes. You could do that then in Washington. It was normal for men to take a couple of hours in the middle of the day, have a drink, and swap stories. A better time.

"POWER HOST TO
POWER BROKERS IN THE
POWER CAPITAL"

New York Times, June 5, 2002

The problem with interviewing Tommy Jacomo, the general manager of the Palm restaurant, is that you can't print about half of what he says. You can't even characterize some of it. A few of his favorite phrases defy euphemism. He's that salty.

This is Mr. Jacomo's thirtieth year at the Palm. He sat at a table near the back one afternoon, mulling over a career as "the most powerful man at the most powerful restaurant in the most powerful city in the world," in the words of his friend William A. Regardie, the magazine publisher. But he began by reminiscing about his first love.

"I always wanted to be a mob guy," said Mr. Jacomo, fifty-eight, who grew up in Queens. "I really thought that's what I was going to do with my life." As a child, he studied *The Big Bankroll,* a biography of the gangster Arnold Rothstein. (The book inspired him to wear garters.) For a while, he ran numbers for local hoodlums, inspiring a lifelong passion for horse racing. "Then I realized I wasn't tough enough. Those guys are tough."

At fifteen, Mr. Jacomo dropped out of school and became a laborer, humping roof shingles up ladders for 80 cents an hour. When he was eighteen, his father (who was head bartender at the Waldorf-Astoria for forty years) got him a bar job at the New York Hilton.

In 1972, he was running the Avalanche Motor Lodge, a motel and nightclub in Vermont. One day, Ray Jacomo, his brother, called to say he was moving to Washington to open a satellite of the Palm in New York and invited him along. Ray Jacomo became the first general manager. (He moved to Miami Beach to open a Palm there thirteen years ago and was replaced by his brother.) Tommy Jacomo built the restaurant's booths with plywood and a hand saw, then became its manager.

All went smoothly until 1977, when he was arrested and charged with arranging the sale of an ounce of cocaine to an undercover officer of the Drug Enforcement Administration. The sale allegedly took place at the Palm. There was physical evidence, including a canceled check and at least one tape-recorded phone conversation. The prosecutor referred to Mr. Jacomo as the "maître d' of cocaine." He faced up to twelve years in prison.

Mr. Jacomo's first call was to Edward Bennett Williams, the criminal defense lawyer, co-owner of the Washington Redskins football team and a patron of the Palm. They were friends—sometimes going together to the fights in Atlantic City—and Mr. Williams mobilized his law firm, Williams & Connolly, in Mr. Jacomo's defense.

"We had a mock trial in Williams's office," Mr. Jacomo remembered. "One of the lawyers starts asking me prosecutor questions. The first one, I reached for a cigarette." By the second question, he was conjugating expletives six different ways. Mr. Williams quickly made a command decision, Mr. Jacomo said: "Tommy will not be taking the stand."

He never spoke in court. The jury acquitted him in an hour.

Now, years later, one of the prosecutors in the case is a Palm regular. Mr. Jacomo is not a grudge holder. In Washington, everybody eats at the Palm—Democrats and Republicans, lobbyists and the lobbied, the defense and the prosecution.

Mr. Jacomo said he doesn't take anyone's side. "I'm Switzerland," he said, refusing to disclose whom he votes for ("Never!") or even whether he votes. "I didn't know anything about politics when I got here," he said. "I learned real fast: keep your mouth shut. And waffle."

He takes the same position about seating: all tables at the Palm are equally good. Eugene J. McCarthy, the former senator and presidential candidate, eats at the front of the restaurant, near William J. Bennett, the author and former drug czar. Robert Bennett, Mr. Bennett's brother, a Washington lawyer who once represented Bill Clinton, usually takes a booth near the back. Larry King sits in the middle of the main room. "There's no Siberia," says Mr. Jacomo, an accomplished diplomat.

The patrons appear to believe it. Many are compulsively regular customers. At 12:30 p.m. last September 11, as thousands fled the city in anticipation of more terrorist attacks, the Palm was at least half full. William Schulz, the chief of the *Reader's Digest* bureau here, was at his usual table. Mr. Schulz has been eating lunch at the Palm four days a week every week for fifteen years. "I like Tommy," he explained. "I like the waiters. I like the atmosphere." Mr. Schulz paused. "And the food's all right."

The crab cakes are superb, but for the most part the food at the Palm is exactly that: all right. Even among Washington steakhouses, it is not the best. (Everyone agrees that the Prime Rib has better meat.) But that is not the point. A city of transients and bureaucrats is not likely to produce interesting restaurants, and Washington has not. The Palm is an exception.

There are no college students on the staff. Most of the waiters are middle-aged married men with children. Many have worked at the Palm more than a decade. The bartender, who is Mr. Jacomo's brother-in-law, has been there for twenty-six years. The head chef, Sang Ek, came to the Palm from Cambodia as a dishwasher twenty-nine years ago. All are famously well paid. (Mr. Jacomo will not say how well paid, but the subject has drawn the attention of the Internal Revenue Service, which in the late 1980s went after waiters for failing to declare a total of $145,000 in tips. Eight of them went to prison.)

At lunch, Mr. Jacomo sipped sparkling water. He didn't eat. He never does when there are customers in the Palm. When you run a restaurant, he said, every day is like Christmas dinner with your Italian relatives. "You're making sure Aunt So-and-so has what she wants and Uncle So-and-so isn't too drunk."

Making sure people have what they want is Mr. Jacomo's true talent. He is a savant with names. He remembers what people do, what they did, where they live, what they like. He can gossip without wounding. And he is accepted as an intimate by many who have very few intimates. At the funeral in 1997 of Jack Kent Cooke, the Redskins co-owner, from which many who had expected to be asked were excluded, there was Mr. Jacomo, front and center.

At times, he and his waiters are called on to deliver the ultimate in customer service. Over the years, they have saved at least ten people from choking to death, a hazard inherent in restaurants that serve solid food in large portions. It is always the same, Mr. Jacomo said: "You give them the Heimlich, they sit back down, get their color back. And then they start eating again. It's amazing."

———

I included this piece mostly as a measure of how much things have changed. In the days before the internet, Who's Who was a trusted reference source. It shouldn't have been. Who's Who was a transparent scam. In other words, it was the Wikipedia of its day, except bulkier and more expensive.

"HALL OF LAME"

Forbes, March 8, 1999

Michael Bolanos made it into Who's Who in America last year. To celebrate, Bolanos, who runs a celebrity-oriented website in New York, fired off a full-page press release to "entertainment and business editors" heralding his triumph. "To be chosen for inclusion," read the release, "candidates must have held a position of responsibility or have attained a significant achievement in their field." Who's Who, Bolanos reminded the editors, is a "guide to today's most influential people."

Congratulations, Mr. Bolanos. Now meet Anita Dawn Sawyer, a fellow influential person of significant achievement who also recently earned a place in Who's Who in America. Sawyer, a 1986 graduate of the University of Central Arkansas, teaches junior high school special education classes in Little Rock. Since 1991 she's coached bowling and floor hockey in the Alpena (Arkansas) Special Olympics. According to Who's Who, her hobbies include cooking, reading, crafts, playing piano, and singing.

Or say hello to Stephen Geiman, who teaches gym at Wilson Memorial High School in Fishersville, Virginia. From 1970 to 1972, Geiman, a graduate of the physical education program at Appalachian State University, was the school's driver's ed instructor. Or David Dolsen, an undertaker in Denver. Or Amy Fung, an accountant from Staten Island. And let's not forget Mary Morgan, a fifty-five-year-old social worker in Elizabethtown, Kentucky. Or Lila Licens, an administrative assistant from Tacoma, Washington, who has been president of the Mount Rainier chapter of Professional Secretaries International since 1994. Or Courtland Paul, a landscape architect in San Juan Capistrano, California, who implores Who's Who readers to "Be on time, produce more than is expected and always, ALWAYS be fair!!!" And of course there's Marguerite Gearhart, a school nurse in Jupiter, Florida, who lists among her myriad accomplishments a 1968–69 stint as "co-leader" of a Campfire Girls troop. Never heard of these people? Then you haven't read Who's Who lately.

Not that anybody has read Who's Who lately, or ever, at least not very closely. The point of Who's Who is not to read it, but to be in it. One hundred years after it was first published by Chicago newspaper publisher Albert Nelson Marquis (who despite his ostensible commitment to accuracy pronounced his name "Markwis"), Who's Who has been a fairly reliable guide to who has made it and who has not. That's been the marketing strategy, anyway. Flip through the latest volume, however, and it's hard not to conclude that something has changed, that the selection criteria for "Honored Biographees" in Marquis's Who's Who have become—how to put it?—more democratic.

Though the number of entries in Who's Who in America has grown to over 100,000 in recent years, the publication has tried hard to convey the impression that standards for inclusion have remained the same. Being accepted into Who's Who is "an honor that only a select few ever enjoy," the company boasts. Every person in the book is subjected to "painstaking selection, research, rigorous nominee review, and thorough editorial review." And who does the painstaking nominating and selecting? Marquis implies that members of the publication's Board of Advisors play a large role in the nomination process, but they don't seem to know much about it.

"The reality is, I don't do anything," says John Fox Sullivan, publisher of *National Journal* and a member of the board for the last decade. "There is almost no communication back and forth. Once a year I get a piece of paper asking me if I want to recommend someone. It's not as if there's an annual retreat somewhere where we sit around and decide who makes it this year. Or if there is, I haven't been invited."

Mindy Aloff, a dance critic whose name is also on Who's Who letterhead, seems to have been left off the guest list, too. "They didn't give us any guidelines for nominating people," says Aloff, who rarely forwards names to the publication.

Then who is making the decisions? Paul Canning, the publication's editorial director from 1992 to 1997, wouldn't give a specific answer, though he did say that the admissions process is relatively simple. According to Canning, in order to become an Honored Biographee in Who's Who in America, the flagship Marquis publication, a person must meet "qualitative and quantitative criteria." An artist, for instance, "will have to have pieces in multiple collections at recognized museums and have one-person shows. For Fortune 500 companies, senior vice presidents and above are listed." Some people, said Canning, make the cut automatically. "We have a thick binder of all the people who must be included, like artistic directors at ballet companies in major U.S. cities, or CEOs of Fortune 1000 companies. We look for writers on the *New York Times* best-seller list. We have Nobel Prize winners, Oscar winners."

Fair enough. But Who's Who in America also appears to contain a lot of relatively unaccomplished people who simply nominated themselves. To make the process of self-promotion easier, Reed Elsevier, the publication's parent company and the owner of Lexis-Nexis, now has a site on the internet where would-be biographees can complete a "biographical data form." Spaces are provided for "career history," as well as for "awards, honors, and grants." Applicants who are uncomfortable with sending personal information over the Web are invited to fax their biographies to a number provided on the screen.

There's not a word about qualitative or quantitative criteria. Does everyone who applies get into Who's Who? "I'll say a majority," admitted Canning, "but I can't get any more detailed than that. I think the majority are appropriate for one of our regional or topical publications. I think I need to leave it at that."

In other words, just about everyone who tries hard enough will get his name in print.

Donald Ray Grubbs of Portland, Texas, is proof that persistence pays off. From 1973 to 1986, Donald Ray worked as a pipe fitter and welder for the Pipefitters Local 195 in Beaumont. Now an employee of Longview Inspection, a company that assesses the structural integrity of industrial sites, Grubbs has been appearing in various Who's Who publications for a decade or so. Only a couple of years ago, he said, was he "elected" to Who's Who in America. "You work up the chain of Who's Who documents," Grubbs explained. "I was in Who's Who in American Education, Who's Who in the World, and then Who's Who in America." When we talked to Grubbs, he had just received a letter indicating that he had been inducted into yet another volume, Who's Who in the South and Southwest. He sounded pleased. "I have nothing but praise to say about them because I think they're serving a good job. People like me who really don't get out there in the limelight, this is one of our ways of getting a little bit of recognition. And it feels good." So good, Grubbs said, that he has purchased a number of Who's Who products over the years, including a commemorative wall plaque. (The plaque, he confided, wasn't of the highest quality.) Yet despite his achievements in the world of Who's Who, Grubbs doesn't put on airs. "I don't profess to be a nationally recognized welding instructor," he said. On the other hand, Grubbs pointed out, neither are a lot of other people in the book. "Probably half of the welding staff at Ohio State University are members of Who's Who."

Nationally recognized welding instructor or not, Donald Ray Grubbs seems like a fairly straightforward person, which is more than can be said for many of his fellow biographees. As most of those listed in the book know, entries in Who's Who are mostly self-reported and largely unchecked, making it the ideal place to tidy up an uneven educational or work history. When Larry Lawrence, the late ambassador to Switzerland, wanted to replace his years at Wilbur Wright Junior College with a degree from the University of Arizona, he turned to Who's Who. Unfortunately for Lawrence, he got greedy, giving himself a membership in a veterans association to back up his spurious war history and a spot on the Nobel Peace Prize Nominating Commission before he was finally caught (though not by Who's Who) and exhumed from his grave at Arlington National Cemetery. Pamela Harriman, another deceased ambassador, never completed college, but claimed in Who's Who to have done postgraduate work at the Sorbonne. To this day, columnist Carl Rowan lists twenty-two different college degrees in his entry, none of them identified as honorary. According to Who's Who, Rowan graduated from three different colleges in 1966 alone, all while working as a syndicated columnist.

Not all attempts at resume-laundering are so blatant, though some are considerably more sinister. In 1995, someone at the Anti-Defamation League of B'nai B'rith noticed that Willis Carto, founder of the lunatic Liberty Lobby, was listed in Who's Who as a "publishing executive." Although the ADL promptly notified Marquis that Carto's publishing ventures consisted of printing anti-Semitic tracts, his entry was not dropped until 1998. ("He never did buy the book," chuckles Carto's spokesman.)

In the mid-1980s, Joe Queenan, then at *American Business* magazine, decided to test the Who's Who fact-checking apparatus. Queenan submitted an application on behalf of a nonexistent magazine editor named R. C. Webster. Webster, Queenan wrote, had graduated with a master of fine arts degree from F&M T&A University and received doctorates from Quaker State University and the University of Ron (Ron, France) before moving on to edit such magazines as *American Business, Latin-American Business, The Business of Business, Your Business,* and *Our Business Monthly.* Webster and his wife, the former Trish Abigail Boogen, had children named Cassette, Lothar, Skippy, and Boo-Boo. A member of the Association of Men and the Bureau of People, he listed his hobby as "managing editing." Who's Who printed most of the entry in its following edition.

It was an embarrassing episode for Marquis, and thanks to improved scrutiny, most of the people listed in Who's Who in America these days almost certainly exist. But the book is still not edited thoroughly, which means that many entries are printed at lengths curiously out of proportion to their importance. Margaret Estelle Vorous, for example, an elementary school librarian in Berkeley Springs, West Virginia, who counts among her achievements being a blood donor, receives 49 lines in Who's Who. Henry Kissinger gets only 34. Anita Dawn Sawyer of Harrison, Arkansas, meanwhile, gets twice the space of Diane Sawyer of ABC News, who is listed three entries down.

Still, with 105,000 biographies, there are bound to be worthwhile tidbits buried in Who's Who in America, and there are. Who, for instance, apart from girls who grew up in the 1980s, knew that Pat Benatar's real name was Pat Andrzejewski? Or that the rap singer Ice Cube was born O'Shea Jackson? And it's undeniably interesting—if a little sad—to learn that *Playboy* founder Hugh Hefner was first married way back in 1949. Other "facts" in the volume make for less scintillating reading.

Indeed, the first clue that Who's Who is a vanity publication is the "Thoughts on My Life" feature that appears beneath some entries. This is the part where biographees are invited to reflect upon their achievements using their own words. It's all pretty amusing, and it must be profitable, too, because Marquis recently decided to expand the concept. For $150, those listed in Who's Who in America can now write up to two hundred words about themselves and their work. A 1997 direct-mail pitch suggests that biographees use the "Enhanced Biography" option to draft their own personal classified ads, sure to be seen by "industry leaders and executive recruiters." "Over 22 years of progressively responsible experience in the food service industry in key decision-making sales and marketing roles," reads one sample entry. "Recent accomplishments include successful product introductions into local markets, which generated $12.3 million growth in annual incremental sales." Perhaps "executive recruiters" really do pore over Who's Who looking to fill highly paid CEO slots. Or perhaps not. Either way, it's hard to see how information like this is valuable to reference librarians, the group for whom the volume is ostensibly written.

That is, until you notice the large number of librarians

who are listed in Who's Who in America. "We think librarians are important," explained Paul Canning. "We think they contribute to society." They are certainly in a position to contribute to Who's Who. The ever-growing Marquis list now includes twenty different Who's Who volumes, including various CD-ROM versions, many of which are updated annually. A single three-volume edition of Who's Who in America can cost more than $500. A three-year subscription to the entire Who's Who product line goes for $5,686. Suddenly it becomes clear how Ruth Ferro-Nyalka, a librarian at the Hinsdale (Illinois) public library, might have breezed through "Marquis' unique and time-proven compilation process" to earn a spot in Who's Who in America.

Which is not to imply that vain librarians are Marquis's only source of income. The company won't say who buys its books, or even how many copies it prints. "I will not elaborate on anything about Who's Who to someone over the phone," said publisher Randy Mysel, brusquely. "A fax won't do it, either." A call to the company's business office proves more fruitful. Who's Who, it turns out, does a pretty good business renting the names and addresses of its 250,000 Honored Biographees to direct mail marketers. People who are listed in Who's Who, Marquis assures marketers in its promotional literature, "are interested in many types of offers," including pitches for new credit cards, magazine subscriptions, catalogs, association memberships and "fundraising opportunities." The entire database can be rented on computer tape for about $22,000. Or, the woman on the phone says, the list can be broken down by profession, sex, political affiliation, or religion. There are 17,600 self-identified Catholics in Who's Who, she explains by way of example, and 5,300 Jews.

It must be a good list, since many Honored Biographees clearly have a weakness for ordering schlocky products through the mail. Marquis makes certain they have plenty to buy. The company's "Reflections of Success" catalog advertises an entire line of Who's Who–related junk, from Who's Who lapel pins (at $52.95 plus shipping and handling, they "quietly declare your accomplishments") to Who's Who key rings, paperweights, and crystal boxes. The home office seems to do a particularly brisk business in commemorative wall plaques, which at close to a hundred dollars apiece doubtless make for a profitable little sideline.

One of the latest offerings from Marquis is the Who's Who/ Chevy Chase Bank MasterCard. Cardholders are eligible for a discount on any merchandise they buy from the Who's Who catalog, which brings the entire enterprise full circle. I'm not listed in any of the Who's Who volumes, but I decided to order one anyway, mostly to see if I could. I could. The moment my MasterCard arrived, I called Who's Who. "One sterling lapel pin, please," I said. "I'm interested in quietly declaring some of my achievements." "Which book are you included in?" the woman asked. None, I said. She didn't seem fazed in the slightest. "Well, you have to be listed," she said brightly. "But you can talk to the editorial department about that. I'll transfer you."

A few days in Appleton, Wisconsin, with Joel Suprise taught me that not all geniuses work at hedge funds. Some of them you'll find sitting in the garage drunk on beer at two in the morning, turning out works of art on home-made lathes. There used to be a lot of men in America like Joel Suprise, guys who could fix and create complicated things with their hands. That's not a romantic view of the past; it's true. Guys like Joel Suprise built the American economy. When manufacturing died, a lot of them drifted off into semipermanent uselessness, getting by on disability payments. Some OD'd on fentanyl. I caught Joel at the last moment in our history before video games and porn gave restless men an easy way to burn energy late at night. When I was with him, Joel was putting his energy into making the world's most advanced potato cannons.

"PRAISE THE LORD
AND PASS THE SPUDS"

GQ, November 2002

There are probably better ways to spend an afternoon than shooting lawn art with a potato cannon, but I haven't tried them. I first did it last summer, while visiting a friend in Maine who sets boat moorings for a living. The mooring business is seasonal, and in the cold months my friend spends a lot of time tinkering in his barn. The winter before he'd built a potato cannon.

Potato cannons are made in virtually every part of the world, but they're particularly popular in communities with bad TV reception and no golf. People with limited recreational options have no choice but to amuse themselves. They read more. They have longer, more meaningful dinner table conversations.

They're far more likely to exploit the explosive properties of underarm deodorant.

Deodorant, like many aerosol-propelled personal grooming products, contains propane. Compressed and ignited, it explodes. If you're looking to turn potatoes into projectiles, Right Guard makes the perfect gunpowder.

So does hairspray. My friend demonstrated. He used a ramrod to force a baking potato down one end of a PVC pipe, sprayed Aquanet into the other end, then capped it. Setting down his drink, he took aim at one of the decorative wooden deer standing guard along the periphery of his backyard. He pulled the trigger, a barbecue igniter set into the underside of the pipe. The cannon roared like a 10-gauge. The deer disintegrated in a haze of potato mist, its birch log legs flying. My friend looked at me and grinned. There were at least a dozen deer still standing. By nightfall we had killed every last one.

Within a week, I had my own potato cannon. Soon I began destroying things at my house. I dented steel trash cans, knocked the limbs off trees, pulverized an eight-foot section of stockade fence. One day I caught myself wondering what effect a potato might have on one of those electrical transformers you see on the top of light poles. It was only a matter of time before I ended up in Appleton, Wisconsin.

Most people know Appleton as the hometown of Joseph Mc-Carthy, Harry Houdini, and the actor Willem Dafoe. Among potato cannon enthusiasts, Appleton is famous because Joel Suprise lives there. Joel Suprise is the owner of the Spudgun

Technology Center, and of its website, Spudtech.com. He makes and sells what may be the most technically advanced potato cannons in the world. But he is more than a successful retailer. He is also an evangelist for the potato cannon movement. Six months from now, when half the people you know own factory-produced, dual-ignition, rifle-barreled potato cannons, you can thank Joel Suprise. He is the Henry Ford of spudgunning.

Like Ford, Joel is an improver rather than a strict innovator. He didn't invent the first potato cannon. No one knows who did. Joel thinks it probably evolved at a backyard barbecue one afternoon many years ago, when someone discovered that if you tape steel beer cans together and add a shot of gasoline, you can fire a potato into the neighbor's yard.

It was a simple concept, but a winning one, and over the years it has been refined by trial and (sadly) some error. When beer cans went to aluminum, spudgun designers went to PCV pipe. At some point, a particularly drunk backyard scientist ran out of potatoes, and entirely new vistas appeared. Potato cannons, it turns out, can be made to fire lemons, apples, squash, pomegranates, plums, Ping-Pong balls, marshmallows, broomsticks, panties, matchbox cars, dirt clods, flaming toilet paper, and chunks of ice. Among many other things. Firing unlikely objects from a length of plumbing pipe is huge fun, something millions of Americans would want to try if they knew they could. This was Joel's insight.

If there was ever a man born to have such an insight, it's Joel Suprise. As a child growing up on a farm in rural Wisconsin, he played with fireworks, tipped cows, and built pipe bombs. In high school, he became obsessed with paintball. Joel constructed his first cannon several years ago, while working in a plant that builds sanitary-napkin-making machinery. The cannon was made of sheet metal and fueled by black powder. It could fire a golf ball over a mile.

That was impressive, for a while. Then Joel got a new job, working third shift as a journeyman electrician at the Neenah Foundry, a nearby factory that makes manhole covers. Neenah Foundry is a union shop (Glass Molders and Plastics, Local 121 B), which among other things means that Joel and his fellow electricians often had free time on the job. "As long as the place is running—nothing's broken down—there's a lot of what we call 'government work.'"

Government work soon produced an imposing new cannon: a 142-pound brushed aluminum artillery piece, with linear bearings and hydraulic recoil suppression. Joel built it in the foundry's machine shop. It looks like a scale-model howitzer. It shoots billiard balls.

Joel's hobby was beginning to get out of hand. It was around this time, in one of those serendipitous meetings of like-minded obsessives, that Joel stumbled upon a website run by a man in Texas named Ed Goldmann. Goldmann had been running a small spudgun business online, and he was looking to sell. Joel consulted his girlfriend, took out a $30,000 home equity loan, and bought it. On July 16, 2001, he became the new proprietor of Spudtech.com.

If Joel Suprise is the Henry Ford of the story, Ed Goldmann is the J. J. Etienne Lenoir. Lenoir, you may not recall, was a brilliant French engineer who built the first workable gasoline engine. For his efforts he was rewarded with anonymity, while the names of those who improved on his design are memorialized on the world's hubcaps. You get the feeling the same sad fate awaits Ed Goldmann.

Or maybe not. It's possible that Goldmann may someday make the news. A doctoral student in chemical engineering at the University of Texas at Austin, Goldmann is currently working on a dissertation titled "Thermoreversible Gelation of Aromatic Hydrocarbons"—or, as he explains, a study of "the physical properties of napalm." He is intense and self-directed. In pictures, he bears a remarkable resemblance to the young Ted Kaczynski.

Like Joel, Goldmann spent much of high school thinking of new ways to blow things up. In college in Washington State, he and a friend made a bet to see who could construct a more powerful spudgun. Goldmann went over the top. He spent $2,000 and created a shoulder-mounted, bolt-action aluminum potato bazooka, fueled by propane tanks carried in a backpack, flamethrower style.

But that wasn't his most important innovation. Goldmann wanted a more accurate spudgun, so he decided to build a machine that could rifle PVC pipe. "I was just bored one day," Goldmann remembers. "I'd heard stories about guys putting nails through broomsticks and twisting them through the bore. That was lame." Once complete, Goldmann's creation was bigger than a Chevy Suburban, operated entirely by pulleys and cranks. It worked perfectly. Over the next couple of years, he sold more than a mile of rifled PVC barrels.

Then he got bored again. After meeting Joel online, Goldmann loaded his inventions into an elderly Dodge pickup and drove to Appleton. Which is how Joel D. Suprise, journeyman electrician, came to posses America's only spudgun rifling machine.

From the outside, the Spudgun Technology Center looks a lot like an ordinary two-car garage, complete with cracked vinyl siding and a 1980 Olds Toronado parked in the driveway. Inside, it is a compact but well-equipped factory. Lathes, drill presses, and grinding machines line one wall. An enormous rack of PVC pipe dominates the other. Scattered around the room are cannons, mortars, bazookas, and rifles in various states of completion. Joel spends a lot of time here, often late at night and often while drinking.

Alcohol seems to unleash Joel's creative forces. "Sometimes when I'm out here with about twelve beers in me, I think of something new," he says. "I was blitzed when I thought of that fucker." Joel points across the room to his latest creation. It's called the Mega Launcher. It is undeniably mega. Its massive sewer pipe barrel is eight feet long, not counting the flash suppressor. The compression chambers are even bigger. At the moment, the thing is bolted to a steel sawhorse, although it can also be mounted on a tripod for better elevation and accuracy. Either way, the effect is martial. The Mega Launcher looks like it was torn from the hood of a Humvee.

It might have been. Stoked to 100 psi with an industrial air compressor, the cannon generates a muzzle velocity of more than 650 feet per second, enough to propel a potato into the next county. Joel sees even greater potential. "You could fill a soda bottle full of sand and blow it through a concrete block wall, to be honest with you."

To be honest with you, I was all for finding a concrete block wall and testing the claim. Joel was, too, but there were practical hurdles. For one thing, it was dark and we'd been drinking. For another, Joel's neighbors were asleep. The Mega Launcher would definitely wake them. We went out to dinner instead.

If he hadn't gone into spudguns, Joel Suprise would have been a great NASCAR driver. Not only does he have the perfect name for it, he looks the part. Joel wears cowboy hats and boots and has a ponytail down to his waist. He chain-smokes Marlboros ("cigarette smoke is about the healthiest thing you're going breathe at the foundry") and drinks Bloody Marys with dinner. Like the most popular drivers, no matter what radical thing he's talking about, he comes off as ingenuous. When Joel says "rock on!" it's not in an ironic Spinal Tap sort of way. He says it like he means it.

Joel lives with his girlfriend, Jane. At thirty-two, she's five years older, and a captain in the Army Reserves. (If she ever gets promoted and marries Joel, she jokes, she'll be Major Suprise.) By day, Jane works at the pharmacy counter at Walgreens. On the side, she runs a small internet business selling quilted baby blankets. Most of the rest of the time, she sits at the workbench watching Joel work. Like Joel, her daily life is framed by the rhythms and demands of potato cannon production. Among her responsibilities is ammunition procurement. "I work near the pet store and the grocery, so it's always, 'Can you pick up some potatoes and tennis balls?'"

The afternoon I arrived, Jane, who was wearing a Marlboro jacket, greeted me at the door with a bottle of beer and a bag of cheese curds, an alarmingly fresh dairy product ("in the cow this morning") that squeaks when they rub against your teeth. Joel was standing at the lathe. A basic potato cannon isn't terribly complicated to make, and even with all the custom features he adds (dual igniters, interchangeable barrels, a potato knife built into the muzzle) Joel can put one together quickly at a relatively low cost. He sells them for about $100 apiece. "His profit margin is obscene," says Jane happily.

Joel's business has been self-supporting since the day he bought it. He has since branched out into parts and accessories. He sells valves and rifled pipe and silencers and laser sights. Lately he has been producing T-shirt and confetti launchers for parades and promotional events. He's working on a contract with the military to develop a gun that shoots grappling hooks.

Within a couple of months of buying the business, Joel's friends at the manhole cover factory stopped laughing at him. This spring, he quit Neenah Foundry for good. He no longer needed the money. Plus, though Joel himself would never say this, it was beginning to seem a little incongruous for a certified cult figure to be working as an electrician.

Spudtech.com draws hundreds of thousands of visitors a month, so Joel gets a lot of email. People write in with all sorts of questions, but generally those who send them fall into one of two categories: aerospace engineers, and demented twelve-year-olds. The former want to chat about chamber-to-barrel ratios, or relative expansion pressures. The latter want tips on destroying things with potatoes.

"Is there a way to add three barrels to make a Gatling gun, or is it possible to add a clip to it?" asks one kid hopefully. "I want to build a 'drive by spudder,'" writes another. "I know it could get me in trouble, but for now I am willing to take the risk. The question I have is, how large to build it? I am thinking about 18 inches or so in total length is going to be just long enough to safely and easily load in the car while driving." He goes on to say that, in his experience, gasoline makes a terrific propellant.

A lot of people write Joel asking about propellants. Right Guard is effective enough to satisfy weekend hobbyists, but varsity spudgunners want more. "There have been guys who've done some really insane shit using acetylene," Joel says. "I get emails all the time asking me about it." Ether, too, produces dramatic effects, as Joel discovered one late night in his workshop. "Ether's pretty aggressive. I shot the clock off the wall with a shop rag."

Joel tries to respond to all of his email, though as a rule he doesn't encourage anyone with starkly obvious criminal intent. It's probably just as well. At the moment, potato cannons are legal and unregulated in most places. (The ATF has determined that they do not qualify as firearms.) That may change. A California state assemblyman named Jay La Seur has introduced a bill that would make possession of a spudgun a felony. Violators could face fifteen years in prison. The Brady Campaign to Prevent Gun Violence has also weighed in, calling potato cannons a "hazard" to civic order. And there's no question that many ordinary citizens, if they knew what midwestern teenagers were doing with PVC pipe, might be concerned. In a recent story about the spudgun "subculture," a Copley News Service reporter described the potato cannon websites he visited as "chilling."

It's true that potato cannons can be dangerous. Peer into the muzzle of a loaded spudgun and you're likely to lose an eye. Several people have. And there can be combustion-related problems. In 1998, three California high school students were injured (one burned over 35 percent of his body and almost killed) when a tennis ball cannon they built in science class blew up on the school's football field. On the other hand, the kids added too much methanol. You've got to use common sense.

It's a point Joel often makes. As a spudgun designer living in a city, safety is an ongoing concern, especially when it comes time to test new products. Joel used to conduct experiments in the scrapyard outside the foundry (he and some friends once proved that it's possible to penetrate a steel oil drum with a wooden dowel). But at home he has to be more cautious. Some of Joel's bigger cannons will fire a can of Mountain Dew eight blocks. Do that too often, he says, "and the chances you're going to kill a four-year-old kid on his bike are pretty high." Bottom line: "It's really hard to do R-and-D work in a residential neighborhood."

Someday, Joel says, he'll build a steel backstop in his backyard. For now, he does most of his research on his parents' farm, forty-five minutes away in Sheboygan. He agrees to take me there, and the next morning we meet at his house to set off.

But first we have a beer. People in Wisconsin take their beer drinking seriously, and Joel more seriously than most. A couch in his living room has a built-in cooler between the seats, which recline and vibrate and have stereo speakers set into the head-rests. A man with a strong enough bladder could watch a whole Packers game on it without moving.

In Joel's case this is purely theoretical, since he can't stop moving. He is filled with energy, a nonstop tinkerer, tweaker, and pursuer of hobbies. Upstairs he has constructed an entire Plexiglas room for his pet eleven-foot python and two boa con-strictors. Once a month or so, he feeds them live rabbits. (Jane doesn't like to watch. "They sound human when they scream," she says.) In the basement he has built a highly complex, elec-tronically controlled still capable of producing 180-proof moon-shine at close to a commercial rate. Joel doesn't sell the booze, or even drink much of it. He just likes to make it.

Finally it's time to go to Sheboygan. Joel and I grab another beer, load up his Dodge Shadow with explosive supplies, and head out. On the way, Joel eats a Wendy's chicken sandwich and talks about some of the more gruesome accidents that have occurred at the foundry over the years.

And then we're there: the Suprise homestead, a sturdy farmhouse framed against a vast expanse of grain silos and dairy cows. Joel's parents are home and waiting for us. Like his son, Joel's father holds his beer and cigarette in the same hand. He seems proud of his boy. "I like guns and hunting," he says, "but Joel takes it to another level."

Everyone pitches in to unload the car. By the time we're done, there's an arsenal laid out on the back lawn: a box of tennis balls, a bottle of propane, a sack of russet potatoes, an entire gross of fluorescent rubber Superballs, as well as six cannons of various sizes and shapes. In the middle of it all is the one I can't wait to shoot: a tripod-mounted harpoon gun. The thing is designed to fire a four-foot aluminum spear tethered to fifty yards of braided steel aircraft cable. Joel made it for a guy in Oregon who claims he wants to harpoon logs that float down the river in front of his house. It's not a very plausible explanation; there are much easier ways to gather firewood. But it's not Joel's nature to ask his customers a lot of probing personal questions, so he hasn't.

Not that it matters now. Joel has come to Sheboygan to test his products, not the motives of those who buy them. First up is a pneumatic tennis ball cannon. Joel sells a lot of these to hunters who use them to train their dogs to retrieve. Joel is confident the cannon will work. But just how powerful is it? To find out, he takes a hypodermic needle from his pocket and injects a tennis ball with 100 cc's of water. He stuffs the ball, now only slightly lighter than a rock of the same size, down the barrel with a ramrod and fires. Pow. It explodes from the muzzle like a .50-caliber machine gun round. By the time it sails over the horizon and I lose sight of it, it's still a hundred feet in the air.

Amazing. And just the beginning of a long, loud afternoon. We shoot tennis balls, rubber balls, and potato after potato. Joel and I try to hit a sheet of half-inch plywood he has erected as target. Joel's father seems to be aiming for the hay wagon. It's cold out, so we retreat to the garage for a break. Hanging from a wall is an industrial-sized roll of maxi-pad bunting that Joel liberated from the plant where he once worked. Joel lights a cigarette and thinks out loud about the harpoon gun. "You know," he says, "if you put a ball bearing in there you could probably shoot down an airplane with it."

Maybe so, though Joel decides to save that experiment for another day. For now, he wants to know if the harpoon gun works correctly. He didn't bring a tripod, so he and I balance the gun across the arms of a Wal-Mart lawn chair. Joel loads the harpoon, lays the cable in a coil at his feet, and prepares to fire.

It's a tense moment. The gun has taken weeks to perfect, but has never been tested in the field. Will it work? No one speaks. Joel's mother, who seems more excited than anyone, looks like she's holding her breath. Joel fires. The harpoon launches, the steel cable snaps the air with a sound like a whip. The aluminum rod flies twenty-five feet and easily punches through the target. It's a success.

Joel's parents run forward to inspect the impact site. His mother beams. His father shakes his head, impressed. "I don't know about logs," he says, "but it works great on plywood." Joel looks almost moved. "Rock on!" he says.

———

Who's the worst person you've ever interviewed? My wife once asked me that. It's a tough question. I've interviewed thousands of people over thirty years. A lot of them have been morally repulsive. For a while, I wrote about crime for a newspaper in Arkansas. That job entailed long conversions with convicted rapists and murderers, some of whom bragged about what they'd done. They were pretty bad. But the absolute worst? That would have to be a tenured law professor from George Washington University called John Banzhaf. He was certainly the most annoying. No one comes close, actually. At least the rapists and murderers in Little Rock had some degree of self-awareness. They didn't think they were saving the world. John Banzhaf, by contrast, claimed to be doing just that, one self-promoting media appearance at a time. Among other acts of fascism, Banzhaf spent quite a bit of time suing people who allowed smoking on their own property. By the end of our interview, I was so irritated with Banzhaf that I lit a cigarette in his office, just to enrage him. It worked.

"BANZHAF'S GAME"

Weekly Standard, November 13, 1995

In June 1993, the *Washington Post* ran a story about a ballroom-dancing school for children called Mrs. Simpson's Dance Class. The article alleged that Mrs. Simpson's, by its invitation-only enrollment policy, had denied proportionally correct numbers of black students the opportunity to join Washington's most prestigious dance lessons. Whether intentionally or not, the story concluded, Mrs. Simpson's had hurt the feelings of a lot of fourth graders and left their parents feeling awkward.

It all might have ended there, except that a Washington-based law professor named John Banzhaf III happened to read the article. Within days, Banzhaf had filed a discrimination complaint against Mrs. Simpson's with the city's Department of Human Rights and Minority Business Development. The dance class, said Banzhaf, is "training future leaders of our society, so the impact of teaching them that discrimination against race and religion is okay is far more serious than a situation involving people who would not have important decision-making roles in society."

A bewildered Mrs. Simpson hired a lawyer. Banzhaf countered with a press conference. Before long, the matter was settled: Though it continued to "vigorously deny" charges of discrimination, Mrs. Simpson's Dance Class was forced to accept an affirmative action program, complete with diversity goals, annual compliance statements, and an independent monitoring body composed of " at least three African-Americans" to hurry along the inclusion process.

Two years later, Banzhaf remembers the event with apparent fondness. "We got a nice settlement from them," he says. And how is Mrs. Simpson's today? Inclusive? Diverse? A glorious patchwork of multihued boxsteppers? Banzhaf pauses, stumped. "It's not one of those things I have followed up, so I couldn't tell you."

Not that it really matters. For John Banzhaf, whether or not a few more black kids learn the foxtrot was hardly the point of the exercise. The point was publicity—getting it, using it. And by that measure, hauling Mrs. Simpson before a human rights commission was time well spent.

In a city teeming with self-promoters, Banzhaf is the Edmund Hillary of publicity mongering. For thirty years, Banzhaf has been issuing statements, holding press conferences, relentlessly flogging the controversy du jour. Along the way, he has taken on dozens of Mrs. Simpsons—murderous corporations, sexist restaurants, greedy dry cleaners. But don't be fooled. There is no ideology at work here. In John Banzhaf's Crusade for a Better America, there is only one cause worth fighting for: seeing your name in print.

In his office on H Street, across from the law school where he teaches several days a week, Banzhaf reclines behind a desk cluttered with press clippings, videos of his television appearances, and copies of his resume, a four-page, thirty-one-point list of "Major Professional Accomplishments." Now in his mid-fifties, Banzhaf is surrounded by photographs taken at various times during his long career. But this is no ordinary Wall of Ego, for the pictures are almost exclusively of him alone. No grip-and-grins with senators or presidents. No family shots. Just Banzhaf, hands placed regally on a stack of legal briefs, or staring off in a dramatic warrior pose. Banzhaf becomes animated as he explains the difference between himself and his fellow George Washington University professors across the way. "I have called my colleagues myopic legal eunuchs for refusing to test their ideas where they can actually have value," he says. "My colleagues will not go and testify on Capitol Hill. They'd rather write these long, introspective bullshit law review articles. Instead of writing law review articles, I will go out and bring legal actions."

Banzhaf's first legal action of note came in the late 1960s, when, as a young Columbia Law graduate, he used the Federal Communication Commission's "fairness doctrine" to force television stations to run antismoking announcements along with their cigarette commercials. It was a heady victory for a twenty-six-year-old son of a fireman from the Bronx. Though he admits he had no special grudge against smokers—smoking was "not even on my list" of concerns, he says—Banzhaf had tasted notoriety and found it ambrosial.

He promptly quit his job in Manhattan, moved to Washington, and started Action on Smoking and Health, an anti-tobacco group. Soon, ASH was keeping him in the headlines with its intemperate press releases, which Banzhaf delivered by hand to local news agencies. "Two hundred years ago brave men and women pledged their lives, their fortunes and their sacred honors to win their freedom," began a typical anti-cigarette missive from 1971. "What will you pledge to prevent the enslavement and death of millions of children, and to defend your right to breathe unpolluted air?"

ASH was also paying the bills. By 1994, the nonprofit group had an annual operating budget of more than $1.1 million, $261,000 of which went to management salaries. Banzhaf refuses to say how much he takes home, though he does concede the number "probably is" between $100,000 and $200,000.

His reputation as a legal bomb-thrower established, Banzhaf joined the faculty at GWU's National Law Center, where he began teaching a course called Legal Activism. (Banzhaf later boasted he had wanted to name it "Sue the Bastards" but was prevented by square university administrators.) Described in the school catalog as instruction in "legal judo" and "guerrilla law," the course gave students academic credit for bringing legal action against people or establishments they believed were engaging in unfair practices. It also taught them how to handle the media, when to talk to reporters, how to hold a press conference. "We didn't have a concept of public interest law as we have today," he says. "Basically, I started that."

The class soon developed a mystique on campus. The professor took to wearing a Superman T-shirt. His car sported a vanity plate that read "SUE BAS."

Together with his students—dubbed "Banzhaf's Bandits"— Banzhaf began filing lawsuits and complaints against dozens of businesses in the city, mostly on grounds of discrimination. Barbers who billed more for women's haircuts were charged with sexism. Rental car companies that would not do business with drivers under the age of twenty-five got slapped with suits for ageism.

For Banzhaf, teaching was one more chance to increase his fame, to pass it on to future generations. "I've turned out more than 120 students, and they're spread around," he explained to Joe Goulden, author of *The Superlawyers,* in 1972. "One day something is going to bug each one of these guys, and he is going to remember what he did in law school. You get a couple of hundred lawyers doing this, and you are going to have a legal revolution in this country."

The kids loved it. As one student explained to *Washington Lawyer,* "I really like this course because it allows you to act like a lawyer before you actually become one."

Kirk Rankin, a former George Washington law student who took Banzhaf's course in 1992, remembers the thrill of finding a suitable target for a lawsuit: "In the first class we sat around in this big bull session and figured out what ideas to pursue. And someone said, 'What about this idea that there ought to be more johns for females at sporting events?' Banzhaf just beamed. He said, 'As far as I know, young lady, that's my idea. I created the potty parity issue.' He was just ecstatic. He was ready to fight for potty parity." Rankin is now a personal injury lawyer.

Banzhaf's efforts didn't stop at questions of toilet fairness. In the early 1980s, the professor and his students went after a number of Washington restaurants on the grounds that requiring men to wear jackets was discriminatory. (The rule did not apply to women.) At a press conference, Banzhaf warned other, not-yet-sued Washington restaurants "not to continue their [dress code] policy or you may be the defendants in the next lawsuit." The case later was thrown out by a district court judge, who described the action as "frivolous and trivial."

Other suits were taken more seriously. In 1989, Banzhaf discovered that dry-cleaning businesses routinely charged more to wash women's shirts than men's. Although dry cleaners countered that women's clothes were more expensive to wash, Banzhaf and his students pressed on, filing complaints against every laundry in Washington, most owned by immigrant Koreans. Ultimately, the businesses were forced to eat the losses and change their billing practices. "It's an unprecedented agreement to make Washington the first major city where there will not be any discrimination from dry cleaners regarding shirts," he exulted. Before it was over, Banzhaf says today, the Korean dry cleaners' association "went through three or four high-powered law firms" defending itself.

In 1993, still giddy from their war against dry cleaners,

Banzhaf and three of his students filed complaints against Washington nightclubs that held "Ladies' Nights," when women were given breaks on drinks or let in free on slow nights. Again, Banzhaf deemed the practice discriminatory. "You won't see signs advertising Black Night or Wheelchair Night or Catholic Night," he pointed out to the *Charleston Gazette,* "but for some reason Ladies' Night is OK." A local weekly that had dared run ads from bars with ladies' nights also found itself hit with a Banzhaf suit. The manager of one targeted night-club seemed confused by the fuss. "This is our way of honoring" women, said the man, an African immigrant. "Maybe I need to learn more about sexism."

When he wasn't using his students to bully the locals, Banzhaf spent his time bullying them on his own. There were plenty of targets. "Every time I'm reading a newspaper," he told the *Washington City Paper,* "every time I'm listening to a news broadcast, somewhere in the back of my mind there's always a little thing saying, 'Is there some way you could do something here? Is there some legal opportunity?'"

Indeed there was. When he found that the city's all-male Cosmos Club was resisting a push to make it admit women, Banzhaf joined the fray, filing a discrimination complaint under the District's Human Rights Act and forcing the organization to change its policy. When he read in a *Washington Post* column that Dulles airport did not provide baggage carts for passengers in its domestic terminal (the airport said it did not have space for a cart dispenser), he filed a complaint under the Americans with

Disabilities Act. He then sent out at least three press releases trumpeting his attack on the airport. And so on.

Meanwhile, Banzhaf's fame grew, as he appeared on countless television shows to talk about the dangers of cigarette smoking and related topics. In one notorious incident, Banzhaf debated professor Ernest van den Haag on the CBS news program *Nightwatch*. When van den Haag lit a cigar to illustrate a point about smoking, Banzhaf tossed a glass of water on him, prompting an on-air melee. Later, in an appearance on *The Morton Downey Show,* Banzhaf bragged about assaulting the elderly van den Haag: "Mort, I threw water on him, and he didn't have the guts to sue me." It was no surprise when Banzhaf made *Washingtonian* magazine's list of 1993's 25 Most Annoying People.

None of his grandstanding earned Banzhaf the affection of university administrators, a majority of whom voted to deny him tenure on his first attempt in the early 1970s. His persistent championing of unseemly causes on campus turned heads as well. Banzhaf, who takes a special interest in nudism and has done legal work in his spare time for a nudist colony in Maryland, wrote a number of opinion pieces for the student newspaper in which he defended pornography against the assaults of feminist and religious groups. Identified in his op-eds as "the director of the Foundation for Unrestricted Carnal Knowledge," Banzhaf treated readers to an explanation of "the swinging philosophy," as well as a detailed critique of stag films. "Most of the female stars of porno flicks are known and portrayed as

women with lusty appetites and prodigious capacity to perform," he wrote in one piece, arguing that X-rated movies do
not degrade women. By contrast, "Virtually every prostitute can
tell you about male customers who pay her to urinate and or
defecate on them or who wish to be paddled or disciplined."
Don't believe it? Doubters, advised Banzhaf, should "visit any
of the city's X-rated movie theaters or porno book stores and
observe with an open mind."

All this should have been an obvious tip to reporters that he
was not an entirely legitimate source for news stories. In fact, the
opposite seemed to be true: the more press releases Banzhaf sent
out—a computer in his office is programmed with the fax numbers of ninety news organizations—the more fields in which he
claimed expertise, the more his name ended up in print. Over
the years, Banzhaf has made it into hundreds and hundreds of
news stories, dozens of them in the *New York Times* alone.

Plug Banzhaf's name into the Nexis electronic database
and wisps of smoke begin to rise from the terminal—the system can barely cope with the enormity of the task. His name
is everywhere: in the *Memphis Commercial Appeal* on Shan-
non Faulkner's arrival at the Citadel; in the *Detroit News* on
race-based congressional districts; in the *Anchorage Daily News*
on the conduct of the FBI in the 1960s; in the *Atlanta Journal-
Constitution* on Clinton's latest Supreme Court nominee; in
the *San Diego Union-Tribune* on the Reginald Denny beating
trial; on the Gannett News Service wire on Paula Jones's anti-
Clinton accusations; in the *Washington Times* on government
radiation experiments.

In 1992 alone, Banzhaf explained Iran-Contra to the *St. Louis Post-Dispatch;* weighed in on cult deprogramming in the *Chicago Tribune;* talked with the Gannett News Service about Ross Perot's bid for president; held a news conference about protecting the homeless in Washington, D.C.; made his debut in *Modern Brewery Age* on the topic of alcohol poisoning; held forth on the House bank scandal in *Roll Call;* talked with *USA Today* about the Noriega trial; and appeared on *Sonya Live* to share his expertise on the subject of child custody cases.

In every appearance, from the *Fresno Bee* to the *Dallas Morning News,* Banzhaf played the expert, on subjects as varied as they are current: Waco. Oklahoma City. Anita Hill. Ollie North. Marion Barry. William Kennedy Smith. In virtually each case, Banzhaf was contacted by reporters after issuing a press release offering his take as a freelance savant. Shortly after the verdict in the O. J. Simpson trial, for instance, Banzhaf sent out press releases touting his expertise on the subject of jury nullification. A number of papers responded. Banzhaf quickly found his name in the *Virginian-Pilot,* the *Tampa Tribune,* the *Albany Times-Union,* and the *Post and Courier* in Charleston, South Carolina, among others.

No news outlet has been more obliging to the publicity-hungry law professor than *USA Today*. Between 1990 and 1994, the paper referred to Banzhaf in an average of 11 different stories a year. On October 15, 1993, Banzhaf hit pay dirt, getting his name into two separate articles on two different subjects— the Reginald Denny trial and cigarette smoking. For the professor, the almost–hat trick was old hat—he'd done the same thing in the same paper four years before. (Nineteen eighty-nine was a good year for Banzhaf generally; he was quoted in 23 different stories in *USA Today*.) Much of *USA Today*'s comprehensive coverage of all things Banzhaf can be traced back to a single reporter named Sam Meddis. Between 1989 and the middle of 1992, Meddis quoted Banzhaf in 19 stories on at least seven different topics. "When you're on deadline," explains Meddis, you look for people who are "quotable" and who return phone calls. Those kind of people, Meddis says, "you call back again. You don't do it consciously."

All the media attention has been good for Banzhaf's stock. Earlier this year, Al Gore and Donna Shalala invited him to debrief them on the subject of Food and Drug Administration regulation of tobacco. "I recognize that publicity is a very valuable tool," says Banzhaf, reflecting on his success. "In many cases, the publicity is as important as the legal action itself. It means that when I make a threat, it's more likely to be taken seriously."

Kirk Rankin remembers his former professor lecturing the class frequently on the value of notoriety. "He said public interest law has its own rewards. The image he used, at least three or four times, was that getting your name and picture in the paper compensates for not having the big, plush corner office and the high-figure income," Rankin recalls. "But he missed the point: If you're not into publicity, who cares if you get your name in the paper all the time?"

True—if you're not into publicity, that is.

James Carville was one person I was certain I'd dislike when I sat down to interview him in the early spring of 1996. Carville was a famous partisan. He ran Bill Clinton's presidential campaign and shamelessly shilled for the Democratic Party. Watching him from afar, Carville struck me as a transparent fraud. What I discovered in talking to him was that James Carville was indeed a fraud, but openly so, in the most honest and genuine way. Over time, Carville wound up one of my favorite people in the world, one of the few friends I've gone to repeatedly for serious life advice. I haven't taken a new job in twenty years without calling him first. James Carville is a genuinely wise man. What a shock that was to discover. Life is full of happy surprises like that, thank God. They more than compensate for the rest.

"JAMES CARVILLE,
POPULIST PLUTOCRAT"

Weekly Standard, March 18, 1996

I t is the afternoon of the Arizona primary, and James Carville is talking on the phone in his office on Capitol Hill.
Dressed in jeans and a T-shirt, his belt unbuckled, Carville is leaning back in his chair with his running shoes on the
desk while a friend brings him up to date on the latest exit poll
numbers from Phoenix. As Carville listens to the news, grinning and grunting into the receiver, his two dogs, Cavalier King
Charles spaniels, explore the corner of the room. The dogs find
an unidentified piece of paper—a memo from the president?
a tax return?—and quickly reduce it to confetti. Carville looks
up calmly. "Stop that," he says, but it's obvious he doesn't really
mean it, and the dogs chew happily on. Their owner smiles and
goes back to his conversation. James Carville is contented.

And why shouldn't he be? Ten years ago, Carville was forty-one and nearly broke, the veteran of a string of losing political races. Hardly anybody outside of a small group of campaign junkies in a few states knew his name. Today he is famous as the architect of the 1992 Clinton victory. His reptilian features are known to millions from television appearances and countless speeches. His second book in two years, *We're Right, They're Wrong,* has just been released by a major publishing house and already is climbing up the bestseller list. Along the way, the man who in 1985 was taking out loans against his life insurance has become a millionaire several times over.

So much success has left little time for old-fashioned political work, but that doesn't appear to bother Carville. Actually, he seems to delight in it. "I'm kind of like Nixon when they asked him why he didn't go to church on Sunday," Carville explains. "Nixon said, 'I've already done that.' Well, I've already run campaigns. I hope I don't have to do it again. But, hey, sometime I might have to. If that's what it takes to earn a living, then I'll do it." In the meantime, though he may advise the upcoming Clinton campaign in some as-yet-undetermined capacity, there will be no more living in motels, no more all-night strategy sessions, no more war rooms. Not if James Carville can help it. America's best-known political operative has joined the plutocracy.

It's probably just as well. With some spectacular exceptions, Carville's relatively brief career as a political consultant (he didn't begin serious campaigning until 1982) has been decidedly spotty. His political work since Bill Clinton's election has yielded some especially choice disasters. In 1993 alone, Carville ran Governor James Florio's nasty but ultimately unsuccessful campaign against Christine Todd Whitman in New Jersey; signed on to help the administration win public approval for the doomed Clinton health care plan; and advised Greece's New Democracy party candidate Constantine Mitsotakis in what turned out to be his upset defeat in that country's national elections. As if that weren't enough, that same year Carville also embarrassed the White House by criticizing NAFTA in a *Washington Post* op-ed and worked for California assemblyman Richard Katz in the Los Angeles mayor's race. Katz came in fourth with 10 percent of the vote.

Even losing campaign consultants make money, and for Carville the defeats weren't entirely wasted time. In 1994, Senator Harris Wofford hired him as a $25,000-a-month consultant in his ill-fated Pennsylvania reelection effort. And Carville and partner Paul Begala still received $300,000 a year for peddling their talents to the Democratic National Committee. Nonetheless, at some point Carville realized that his future lay in hiring himself out not to campaigns, but to audiences.

He started giving speeches. Lots of them.

It was the money bet. It's arguable that Carville's most marketable asset has always been his eccentric personality. Manic and witty, Carville became legendary among coworkers for his unpredictable, superstitious behavior during campaigns, most famously for refusing to change his undershorts during the final week before an election. During the Lautenberg Senate race in New Jersey, one friend told the *Washingtonian,* Carville was known "to lie on the couch in the fetal position wearing brown gardening gloves. No one knows why."

It's hard to tell to what degree Carville's odd behavior is a part of a sales shtick, but it is clear he cultivates his public image as an unusual and folksy guy. During the 1980s, Carville tells reporters, he helped to found the Washington chapter of the Andy Griffith Rerun Fan Club. Along with the usual polemics, his new book contains recipes for barbecue and "Carville's Top Five Potato Salad Tips." And though he is now a burgher in good standing, Carville plays up his small-town roots, often making surprisingly self-aware and at times nauseatingly cute references to the Louisiana hamlet where he was raised (Carville, Louisiana, home of a federally funded leper colony), his mother "Miss Nippy," and the country store "my daddy had." The facts may be true, but like everything Carville says, they've been spun. "It's a great hook," he once explained, "this crazy Cajun guy, just in from the swamps, who probably bites the heads off moccasins. If my name were Bunky Auchincloss or Sam Greenfield, I'd be just another guy in Washington."

As it is, Carville is a novelty act to his audiences, like a circus performer with political insight. Or, as a close friend suggests, a comedian: "He knows people want to hear a little bit about politics, but basically they want to hear jokes about politics. And that's what he's good at telling. He is an entertainer. That's what he's making money on."

A ton of it. Carville has boasted to acquaintances that he has given two hundred speeches over the past three years. The appearances add up fast. Carville won't specify how much he has made from the lecture circuit—"I can't imagine why it would be anybody's business," harrumphs the man who once made a living digging into his opponents' personal lives—but it's apparent Carville isn't kidding when he says he's been fortunate. A couple of years ago, Carville's booker, the Washington Speakers Bureau, accidentally sent his annual earnings form to another speech-giver with a similar last name. The form, the recipient was shocked to discover, indicated Carville had made more than $900,000 in speaking fees in a single year. If Carville had had his way, it would have been more. According to his agent, Carville receives $15,000 a speech, plus first-class airfare and hotel accommodations. "He's consistently trying to raise it," says the agent, "but we say, 'No, keep it where it is.'"

By all accounts an unusually skilled speaker, Carville jets around the country nearly every week to meet new audiences. "I give a lot of speeches," he admits. "Last night I gave a speech to the *Forbes* magazine people. Sunday it was—what?—Orlando for the National Grocers [Association]. And I'm the commencement speaker at the University of Virginia this year." Other paying customers include Aetna insurance, Seagram's, Citibank, Prudential, and the National Organization of Investment Professionals. Asked if there are any groups he wouldn't speak to, Carville pauses, evidently confused by the question. "I don't know, give me an example," he says. How about International Paper, or some other corporation reviled by liberals for pulping old-growth forests or otherwise despoiling the environment? A grin spreads across his face: "I've probably spoken to them."

If Carville affects nonchalance about his efforts to make

money, he is equally direct about how he spends and manages it. As he explained to *Vanity Fair* a couple of years ago, "My populism doesn't extend to my choice of hotels." And indeed it doesn't. Carville is a bon vivant of the 1940s variety. A wine aficionado (northern Rhônes are his favorite), Carville once consumed no fewer than eleven drinks in the company of a reporter on a flight to Los Angeles. He and his wife (former Bush partisan and talk-show host Mary Matalin) have what he calls a "country house" in rural Virginia. He enjoys quality room service, plush bath towels, and cars that come with drivers. He's a frequent patron of the Palm, one of Washington's most expensive restaurants. And, as if to make the caricature complete, he loves to play the stock market.

In 1994, Carville gave an enthusiastic interview to *Smart Money* magazine in which he outlined his investment strategies. He begins by following the market closely. "You're not supposed to look at the stock tables every day," Carville said. "Not only do I look at the tables, I look for the symbols of the stocks I own running across the screen all day long." That is, when he's not ringing up his stockbroker, something he does "an average of three times a week."

None of this should come as any surprise. Eating big lunches and chatting with the broker is, after all, what wealthy people do, at least in the movies. Still, such admissions do seem odd coming from Carville, who made his reputation—and, ironically, his fortune—by attacking the very people he now brushes elbows with at the Palm. Never comfortable with social issues (a Catholic, he seems squeamish about the liberal positions on abortion and homosexuality), Carville has instead made soaking the rich the guiding theme of the notoriously hardball campaigns he has run. As he put it in a particularly restrained moment to *Campaign* magazine, "Most people don't think the rich pay enough."

Carville has been an especially energetic mouthpiece for liberal populism, particularly the idea that in the American economy the cards are stacked against the Little Guy and it's high time government did something about it. For Carville, the graduated income tax is at the core of what makes America great, the tax rate on capital gains nonnegotiable (though privately he admits indexing them for inflation seems like a pretty good idea). In his latest book, Carville the stock market junkie goes on at some length about how the country is in trouble because "almost all the productivity gains are going into corporate profits" rather than workers' paychecks. "This is not a good sign, to say the least."

For an unabashed populist, however, Carville can seem a little touchy when questions arise about his own financial circumstances. Take for instance the case of Representative Fred Heineman of North Carolina. Heineman, a former police chief from Raleigh, has come in for repeated abuse from Carville, both on television and in print. In his latest book, Carville gives Heineman the first spot on his list of the "Top Five Ridiculous and Pathetic Republicans." Heineman's crime? He once described himself as "lower middle class." And this from a man, scolded Carville, whose "annual income is round about, oh, say, $180,000."

Statements like this beg the question: of what class does Carville consider himself a member? For once, Carville is at a loss for a snappy answer. "Me?" he asks, stalling for time. "I wouldn't describe myself as upper class." Then, gathering his wits and putting on his thickest bayou accent, Carville does what he does best—go on the offensive. "I would describe myself as having a healthy income," he says, his voice rising, "but I sure wouldn't describe the son of a postmaster and an encyclopedia saleswoman as upper class, by any stretch of the imagination. I would describe myself as decidedly middle class. I think I'm extremely fortunate."

That seems to settle the matter, and Carville quickly changes the subject, but the exchange clearly has bothered him. A few days later he calls back to clarify his position on which class he belongs to. He may make a lot of money, he explains in an agitated voice, but that doesn't mean anything. "Larry Flynt is hardly upper class," he says, referring to the pornography publisher, "but he's certainly upper income, and that is the distinction that I make." He then launches into a disjointed accounting of his humble origins, his working-class relatives, his brother-in-law who runs a bowling alley. "My brother-in-law and I are of the same class," he says. Plus, he's really not that well-off. After all, he explains, "My wife works."

To be fair, Carville isn't the first person to insist there's a difference between living like a rich guy and actually being one. Most senators do it every day. Just the same, even a man used to the relentless double-speak of political life is bound to have difficulty balancing economy-class rhetoric with an Admirals Club lifestyle for long, and Carville is no exception. But give him points for effort. When members of the Hotel and Restaurant Workers' Union went on strike at the Palm last fall, Carville took pains to show his solidarity. "I never crossed any picket lines," he says with apparent pride. Of course, that didn't mean he skipped lunch. Carville simply called ahead. When the picketers left, he showed up for steak.

Even a would-be Louisiana populist has his limits, however. Carville apparently reached his the day Paula Corbin Jones held a press conference to announce her sexual harassment suit against President Clinton. Asked for comment, Carville immediately assumed his nastiest campaign persona. "You drag $100 bills through trailer parks, there's no telling what you'll find," he said, sounding more like a snobbish old woman by a country club pool than a defender of the exploited classes. "I know these people. I went to school with them. I necked with them in backseats. I spent nights with them." But apparently he does not identify with them. Not anymore. Carville came close to admitting as much to the *Chicago Tribune* earlier this month. "I may have lost a bit of contact with the rest of the country," he explained with his characteristic mixture of bluntness and spin, "but compared to others who came before me, it's not so bad."

Certainly it's not so bad for Carville, whose latest project—again following the lead of so many others who came before him—is turning his celebrity into a lucrative career as an author. It worked before. His first book, a gossipy semi-autobiography he wrote with his wife, earned the couple a $950,000 advance and became a bestseller. His new volume, an extended paperback screed Carville calls "pamphleteering," brought him a much smaller advance, which he describes derisively as in "the low six figures." Still, the pay's not bad for 160 pages of aggressive opinions in big type. Plus, being an author again gave Carville cause to indulge one of his favorite pastimes: heading to the Palm for lunch, this time with famous people like Norman Mailer to discuss which policies best help the poor.

Carville began *We're Right, They're Wrong* with low hopes— "If you can't read this thing on a moderately long airline flight, I'll be pretty disappointed," he told the *Washington Post* before starting out—and there are few surprises within. The alert consumer opens the covers, pen in hand, ready to catch misstatements, exaggerations, and falsehoods as they may appear. The task quickly proves impossible, simply too enormous to undertake. Before long, the reader feels like an English teacher grading a paper turned in by a dyslexic—the margins fill with exclamation points, corrections, dozens of bewildered question marks. Better to ignore the details, one soon realizes. This thing clearly wasn't meant to be taken literally.

But it is not the errors in the book that stick in the mind, it's the tone. *We're Right, They're Wrong* is so partisan and cant-filled that months before it was published it reportedly caused a feud between Carville and Clinton adviser Dick Morris, who considered it too polemical and therefore bad for the president. (Clinton, for his part, likes the book so much he's taken to citing it in speeches.) It starts right at the beginning, when readers learn that "It's them [Republicans] versus us [Democrats]. Ours is the morally superior position. We're right, they're wrong."

Very wrong, it soon becomes clear. According to the book, Republicans aren't merely "greedy," "inexcusably hypocritical," "unpatriotic," "malicious," "criminally stupid" "terrorists" who would sell poison hamburgers to children in order to pay "off their own campaign IOUs to the meat industry." No, they're worse even than that. Republicans, according to Carville, are monsters who actually enjoy hurting the weak and poor. And, like all truly evil people, they achieve their wicked ends not through democratic means, but by conspiracies.

For example, Carville writes that during the Reagan years (a period described as "a god-awful disaster that we're not going to recover from anytime soon"), a "powerful minority got richer. The rest sat there waiting for trickles of prosperity that never came." So far, so ordinary. Here's the twist: According to Carville, "that result was no accident. It was the game plan all along!" "The truth is," Carville says, that Republicans "believe in comforting the comfortable and afflicting the afflicted." With this in mind, it's not surprising, as Carville asserts, that "right-wingers don't want public education to succeed." Or that the "Contract with America is a direct assault on black people. Period." Or that Republicans "are washing their hands of all responsibility for anybody but well-to-do white folks."

Heavy stuff. It's one thing to accuse a political opponent of neglect or wrongheadedness, quite another to charge the other side with actively seeking to injure the downtrodden. This doesn't sound like the generally measured rhetoric of the schmoozing, socially bipartisan Washington insider James Carville has become.

And, as it turns out, it's not. James Carville didn't actually write the book. Then again, to his considerable credit, he doesn't claim he did.

When it comes to ghostwriters, Carville is no Hillary Clinton. He offers no stories about nights spent writing out chapters in longhand on legal pads or the pain of the "editing process." If Carville does not display an intimate familiarity with his own work that's because, as he puts it, "Lowell's the one who really put the book together. He really did the book."

That would be Lowell Weiss, a twenty-eight-year-old staffer at the *Atlantic Monthly* who, along with at least four other researchers and two editors, assembled *We're Right, They're Wrong*. It took the group about seven months to accomplish the task. Like a campaign, the process of transforming tape recordings of bull sessions with Carville into a readable manuscript required more than a few all-nighters. "Believe me, I did a little bit of everything," says Weiss. "Definitely, when you're with James, you have a full-life commitment to him. It's a lot of work. He's a demanding guy. Most of all, he demands loyalty."

And apparently returns loyalty, as well. Carville is a hero to the many people, most of them young, who work for him. "He's a cult figure," Weiss says. And no wonder. When Carville appeared on *The Tonight Show* to flog his book, he flew his stable of research assistants, including Weiss, out to Los Angeles, put them up in a hotel, got them backstage passes, and took them out to dinner afterward.

What he didn't give them was cover billing. Carville "took a very large risk on hiring me," Weiss says, sounding grateful. "I know he interviewed a number of very, very quality people, probably a number of people who are brighter than I am, better writers and have a lot more experience. And a number of them just insisted in the first couple minutes of their interview, 'I'd like my name on the cover.'" That, apparently, was it for them. As usual, it is Carville himself who says it best: "If I were the kind of person who put justice before ego," he writes in the book's acknowledgments, "Lowell's name would be on the cover of this book with mine."

But it's not, which is too bad for Carville, since the ostensible author might want to share the blame with someone else for some of the whoppers that made it into *We're Right, They're Wrong*. In one of the book's most memorable vignettes, for instance, Carville describes the time he gave the commencement address at Louisiana State University. Carville, according to the book, arrived at the podium to speak, only to realize he had left his speech in the hotel room. True to form, however, he winged it, firing off some of his trademark self-deprecating one-liners even as he laid down some serious profundities.

Great story. But is it true? Well, says Carville sheepishly, "No, it's kind of . . ." He trails off, then quickly changes the subject to a story about Clarence Darrow.

It is in many ways the perfect Carville comeback, if only because Clarence Darrow is the perfect Carville hero: flamboyant, nasty, friend to rogues and underdogs, a man who was himself once tried for bribery. This is the kind of person Carville admires. Spend an hour with James Carville and you're not likely to hear much mushy liberal blather about Shining Tomorrows or why-can't-we-all-just-get-along platitudes. Nor is he likely to bring up his favorite federal programs, a topic explored at eye-glazing length in *We're Right, They're Wrong*. Instead, he is apt to recount anecdotes about some of America's most controversial, and sometimes repugnant, political figures. George Wallace. Ronald Reagan. Earl Long. Pat Buchanan. The only politician to be honored with a photograph in Carville's office is a mustachioed man in a hat and dark glasses named A. O. Rappelet, an old-time Louisiana politician who was eventually booted out of office and ended up, briefly, in jail. Carville may not like them all, but that hardly seems the point. He respects them for their political ability, as one professional to another. And that most definitely is the point. With Carville, you can get the feeling it's the only point.

Which is part of what made Carville a successful campaigner—and what makes him such a wonderful plutocrat. As Carville once said, ideology is "wherever my clients are."

This principle was on full display one night late last month when Carville made an appearance on *Larry King Live*. Dressed in a Yale-cut navy blazer, a blue button-down oxford, and a red and gold rep striped tie from Brooks Brothers, Carville didn't really look himself, but in this environment that hardly mattered. King loved him anyway, proclaiming the author "one of my favorite people." Carville did his usual routine, firing off a few zingers about Republicans, throwing out some pointed statistics about the federal government, taking the requisite call from Cedar Rapids. Before long the show was over, and King turned to his guest to send him off.

"See you at the Palm," said Larry. "Thank you, sir," replied James.

Probably no story I ever did changed my views more than a trip I took to Iraq for Esquire *magazine in 2003. I arrived a tepid supporter of the war, and of neoconservatism more generally. I returned home a determined opponent of both. The reality of Iraq bore no resemblance to the debates we were having back in Washington. The occupation was so clearly a disaster, even early on. The problem wasn't simply that the Iraqi resistance was more determined than we'd imagined, and the country itself more complicated, though both of those things were true. The problem was that America wasn't suited to be a colonial power. Effective colonialists rule the countries they conquer. They bring order and clarity. They make certain they benefit from the exercise of their power, because otherwise, what's the point? America was totally incapable of any of that. The Americans occupying Iraq couldn't even admit to themselves they were colonialists. Instead, the State Department dressed up the whole operation like it was a kind of armed sensitivity training seminar, designed to liberate Iraqi women from their traditional gender roles: "Now that we've overthrown Saddam, we march ahead to overthrow the patriarchy!" The result was failure, accompanied by chaos on every level. Watching it, I realized that there was nothing conservative about neoconservatism. The neocons were just liberals with guns, the most destructive kind. The upside of the trip was that I made a lifelong friend. To this day I'm close to Kelly McCann, the retired Marine officer who guided me in Iraq. He's still one of the most impressive people I know.*

HIRED GUNS

"INSIDE THE (NOT-SO-) SECRET ARMIES OF OPERATION IRAQI FREEDOM"

Esquire, March 2004

About a hundred yards into Iraq, we stopped to pick up weapons. A half-dozen Kurds in white Citroëns met us in a trash-strewn lot just over the border from Kuwait. They were unloading the guns onto the trunk of one of their cars as we pulled up. The pile amounted to a small armory: German MP5 submachine guns, AK-47s newly liberated from the Iraqi army, 9mm Beretta pistols, and dozens of magazines of ammunition.

Just a few feet away, American soldiers stood by the side of the highway directing convoys of fuel trucks heading north. They must have noticed the cluster of men in plain clothes arming themselves with automatic weapons. They didn't acknowledge it. No one demanded to see our identification or weapons permits. No one even asked what we were doing. By local standards, what we were doing was normal. Only a moron drives to Baghdad unarmed.

There were no morons in our convoy. These were American civilian contractors, employees of one of the private security companies the U.S. government has hired to pacify and reconstruct postwar Iraq. The group was led by Kelly McCann, a forty-five-year-old former Marine officer and security expert who also works as an analyst for CNN. McCann and I have been friendly for a couple of years. When I asked him what exactly civilian contractors were doing in Iraq, a subject about which there has been much speculation but relatively few published facts, he offered to show me.

I'd already gotten part of the answer earlier that morning. At 6:30 a.m., eight of us had gathered in a hotel suite outside Kuwait City for a briefing on our drive to Baghdad. Apart from me, everyone in the room was working for DynCorp International, an American firm that specializes in high-risk contract work for the Pentagon and the State Department. Pick an unsafe country and DynCorp is likely to be there. In Afghanistan, DynCorp bodyguards protect Hamid Karzai, the most imperiled president on earth. In Colombia, DynCorp pilots fly coca-killing crop dusters slow and low over drug plantations, an integral part of Washington's Plan Colombia. DynCorp is in Kosovo, Israel (three of its employees were blown up and killed in Gaza last year), East Timor, Sarajevo, Saudi Arabia, the Philippines, Liberia, and many other sketchy places. Last spring, DynCorp—

along with Kroll Inc. and as many as twenty other large private security companies, and perhaps dozens of smaller ones, employing tens of thousands of individual contractors—came to Iraq.

Less than a month after U.S. troops occupied Baghdad, DynCorp won a $50 million contract from the State Department to help instruct the country's police and prison guards in the use of modern, non-torture-related law-enforcement techniques. (All told, the State Department and the Pentagon have issued contracts worth more than $2 billion for security work in Iraq.) DynCorp set about hiring close to a thousand American cops to move to Iraq and accompany their Iraqi counterparts on the job. The pay was good—up to almost $155,000 a year, most of it tax free, plus full expenses—but Iraq is a dangerous place to live. So dangerous that DynCorp also had to hire security contractors, many of them veterans of elite special operations units in the U.S. military, to keep the cops from getting killed once they got there.

I was going to Baghdad with the security contractors. Once we arrived, they'd spend most of their time tightening security around two hotels in the city, the Gardenia and the Baghdad, which housed the American policemen and other DynCorp employees. Both places were obvious targets for Iraqi insurgents. Both had been attacked repeatedly, the Baghdad Hotel with a devastating suicide bombing a few months before. Kelly McCann had come to check up on the work his men were doing and to bring them several cases of security and surveillance gear they couldn't get in Iraq.

At the moment, though, everyone in the room was focused on simply getting to Baghdad. Commercial flights into the city had been suspended after a series of surface-to-air-missile attacks, one of which blew a chunk of a wing off a DHL cargo plane. The overland route was now the only option. It wasn't a great option. In the previous three months, at least nine civilian contractors had been killed in the Nasiriyah area alone. Through which we'd be driving. Hence the briefing.

A former Special Forces sergeant named Jack Altizer set his laptop on a coffee table and began a PowerPoint presentation on all the things that could happen to us on the way. He spoke like a man who'd taken dangerous trips before. His language was crisp and technical, like an NTSB spokesman after an airplane crash. The primary threat, he explained, would come from improvised explosive devices hidden by the side of the road. Typically, an artillery shell, or a series of them daisy-chained together, would be buried under rocks and detonated by remote. He clicked the mouse and an image appeared on the screen showing the result. It was an aerial shot of the aftermath of a recent ambush. The vehicle, an SUV very much like ours, had been pulverized. Even from a distance, you could see that whoever had been in it must be dead.

Not that the attackers took chances. "They cleaned it up with small-arms fire," Jack said. "Cleaned it up" meant "unloaded AK-47s into the bodies."

The briefing went on like this for half an hour. It wasn't clear just who the attackers might be—carjackers, Al Qaeda, Baath Party loyalists, or some combination of the three—only that they had been hurting a lot of Western motorists in recent weeks. Lately there had been reports of attacks from snipers, rocket-propelled grenades, and fixed-place machine guns as well as car-to-car drive-by shootings, ambushes at phony government checkpoints, and hand grenades lobbed through windows in traffic.

And that was just part of what could go wrong on the highway. There was always the possibility that jumpy coalition forces might fire on us, as the 82nd Airborne had done two weeks before to a food-for-oil convoy on the road to Jordan. Small children might run out in front of our vehicle. Or we might simply have a fatal car wreck.

The last scenario didn't seem far-fetched. To make the SUVs harder to hit, we'd be traveling fast, between 110 and 120 miles per hour the whole way, including, if possible, through towns. "Pretty much for no reason will we stop," Jack said. "Drivers, if you're disabled in the kill zone, stay off the brakes. We'll ram you out of there." In other words, even if you've been blown up, be prepared to keep moving. With that, he closed his laptop and we were off.

I was anxious about the border crossing. Before we'd left the United States, I'd heard that some sort of visa or stamp or other official-looking document might be required to enter Iraq. I'd never managed to get one. As it turned out, no one cared. The American soldier standing at the border just nodded at the vehicles and waved us through. We rolled across doing 30.

A moment later, we made our pit stop for guns. I was busy scribbling in my notebook when one of Kelly McCann's men, a former Marine sniper named Shane Schmidt, walked over with an AK-47. Do you know how this works? he asked. I nodded. The week before, Kelly had shown me the basics on his firing range. (Designed by the Soviets to be effective in the hands of teenaged peasants, the Kalashnikov is not a complicated weapon.) Schmidt handed the gun to me. "Take care of it," he said. "If we get hit, don't panic. Collect your thoughts and shoot back."

He stepped back a foot and narrowed his eyes, sizing me up to see if I was the sort of person who might start pulling the trigger indiscriminately once trouble started. "Select your fire. You've got sixty rounds of Iraqi-made ammunition. That's it. Make each one count." I said I would, then racked a cartridge into the chamber, pushed the selector to safe, and got in the car.

Under ordinary circumstances, I would have been reluctant to accept the rifle. I'm not uncomfortable around guns—I've hunted for most of my life—but bringing them on stories is considered taboo. Journalists typically don't carry weapons, even in war zones, for fear of compromising their status as neutral observers. If you're armed, the theory goes, other armed people will consider you a target. Sounds reasonable, except that in Iraq, journalists are considered targets anyway. Thirteen of them were killed there in 2003. All apparently were unarmed. Carrying a gun doesn't make you safe. But it can make you safer. That was enough for me.

Less than an hour into the drive, we got the first sign that someone was watching us. One of the Citroëns in our convoy radioed to say that a pickup truck was coming up from behind extremely fast, even faster than we were going. Jack Altizer had already picked up transmissions on his surveillance gear indicating that two people nearby were communicating on walkie-talkies. It looked like the classic setup to a carjacking: spotter by the side of the road sees Westerners in a convoy; gunmen in a chase vehicle pull up alongside and force them off the road. Or just shoot them.

I was riding in one of the SUVs, a mud-splattered Nissan, in the backseat behind Kelly and Bill Frost, another former Marine. Kelly and I were talking about the approaching pickup when suddenly it appeared right next to us.

There were three young Arab men inside. They were inches away from our driver's-side window, maintaining our speed and giving us hard looks. Kelly's voice never changed its tone. He raised his MP5 off his lap, extended it across Bill's chest, and pointed the muzzle at the men in the pickup. They hit the brakes hard, disappearing into our rearview mirror. Bill never took his eyes off the road. Kelly kept up the conversation as though nothing had happened.

Just south of Nasiriyah, we stopped for gas. Despite having one of the world's largest oil reserves, Iraq has relatively few filling stations. Thanks to sabotaged oil pipelines and a huge glut of new vehicles (more than 300,000 since the war), every station has a gas line. Some are more than a mile long. People can wait for days, camped out in their cars, for a full tank. We had no intention of doing that. Waiting in line, stationary and exposed, was simply too dangerous. Instead, we commandeered the gas station.

All four vehicles roared in at high speed. Two went directly to the pumps. Two formed mobile roadblocks near the entrance. Contractors with guns jumped out and stopped traffic from coming in. Others took positions around the perimeter of the station. Kelly motioned for me to stand guard with my rifle by the back wall. There was a large and growing crowd around us. It looked hostile.

And no wonder. We'd swooped in and stolen their places in line, reminding them, as if they needed it, of the oldest rule there is: armed people get to do exactly what they want; everyone else has to shut up and take it.

It wasn't until later, after we'd left the gas station and were back on the highway, that I felt guilty about any of this. Kelly, to his credit, felt bad, too. There had been quite a few children there. I'd seen them watching as we forced their fathers out of the way to get to the pumps. "We neutered their dads," Kelly said. He was right. We had. And we'd had no choice. It was horrible if you thought about it.

I didn't have a chance to think much about it. We were doing 120 again, weaving between buses and fuel trucks as if they were traffic cones. Bill was at the wheel, chaining Wint-O-Green Life Savers and staring straight ahead. Bill was one of the largest human beings I had ever seen. A former Force Recon sergeant, he had a chest so broad, it seemed impossible. The ceramic plate on the front of his body armor looked like a postage stamp on a balloon. Kelly called him Barney Rubble. He was a remarkable driver.

Coming into a turn on the main drag through Nasiriyah, we

hit an oil patch doing about 70. Suddenly we were off the road, sliding sideways. Through my window I watched transfixed as a building approached at high speed. I could see spidery cracks in the concrete walls, tiny chinks in the wooden door frame. We are going to wind up inside it, I thought. But somehow we didn't. At the last possible second, we shot back across the pavement, onto the dirt divider. Oncoming cars swerved away. Then we came back. And forth. And then we kept going, through downtown Nasiriyah, up onto curbs, into the opposite lanes, screeching through traffic circles, blaring the horn, and barely slowing down. It was thrilling. And no doubt deeply offensive to every other living thing within a ten-mile radius. But there wasn't time to ponder that.

I spent the rest of the trip to Baghdad watching out the window for people making sudden movements. Apart from its dangers, much of Iraq isn't very interesting to look at. The landscape is flat and dun colored. The dirt just beyond the highway is littered with hunks of twisted and mangled metal, some of it the detritus of wars, some of it just unclaimed junk. The countryside looks muddy and broken. Fires from the burnoff of distant oil refineries give the horizon a hazy, sinister look. It's not an appealing place.

Outside of the heavily fortified—and relatively safe—U.S.-controlled "Green Zone" that surrounds Saddam's former main palaces in Baghdad, you can spend days without hearing English or seeing an American flag. Almost nowhere is there the faintest whiff of American cultural influence. People light up in elevators and carry Kalashnikovs to the dinner table. Gunfire and explosions are background noise. It is a place with almost no Western-style rules. It's not a bit like Denver.

You'd think it would be. According to the Pentagon, there are more than 100,000 U.S. troops stationed in Iraq. The country seems to have swallowed them. We drove from the Kuwaiti border to downtown Baghdad and back again and didn't see one on the way—more than seven hundred miles on major roads without catching a glimpse of a single American in uniform.

If the goal is to control the country, there are not enough American forces in Iraq. If the goal is to rebuild it, there could never be enough. The U.S. military simply doesn't have the manpower. As it is, the Pentagon could not fight even a small war without the considerable help of civilian contractors. In Bosnia during the peacekeeping mission, there was at times one contractor for every soldier. That was nearly a decade ago. The military has grown smaller since and even more dependent on contractors. On the battlefield, contractors cook soldiers' food, deliver their mail, provide their housing, and take care of their equipment. (DynCorp maintains virtually all U.S. military aircraft in the Middle East.) In Iraq, they are sometimes nearly indistinguishable from soldiers.

Civilian contractors have been hired to destroy captured Iraqi weapons, clear unexploded ordnance from military bases, transport armored vehicles into the country, and train the new Iraqi army. This in addition to vast logistical support (providing water, power, and fuel to U.S. troops), as well as every sort of humanitarian task, down to providing pencils and rulers to Iraqi schoolchildren.

It's a fruitful arrangement for both parties. In the long term, contractors are cheaper to use than troops, at least theoretically. (Civilian contractors won't be clogging the VA system thirty years from now.) Many of them are good at what they do. And they free soldiers to do what soldiers do best. With civilians handling a portion of the logistics, the Pentagon can focus on the purely combative elements of war fighting—though as it turns out, these civilian contractors do some of that, too.

For the contractors, the allure is simple: generous pay. The work can be risky and uncomfortable, but the money is good. An experienced security consultant willing to live in unruly places can make $250,000 a year in Iraq. For a man coming from a career in the service, as almost all contractors who handle security are, this is a colossal step up. Plus, there is no one around to make you spit-shine your shoes. As Dave Smith, a former British soldier who has worked as a contractor all over the world (including, for a time, in Liberia, for the now-deposed war-criminal president Charles Taylor), put it: "The difference between a contractor and a military guy is I'm getting paid five times as much and I can tell you to get fucked if I don't want to do it." For a certain sort of person, it's a great gig.

The problem is finding that sort of person. Carrying an automatic weapon in a third-world country, beyond the easy reach of higher authority? The job description is like a bug light to borderline personalities. Big companies like DynCorp have every incentive not to hire flakes and compulsive danger seekers. The bad publicity isn't worth it. But in a situation like Iraq last year, in which the federal government threw hundreds of millions of dollars at reconstruction companies, which in turn rushed in thousands of new security contractors, the screen could not be very fine. There are civilians toting guns in Iraq who shouldn't be.

Some of them are easy to spot. I ran into one late one night outside the Gardenia Hotel, a dumpy former office building. Kelly and I were staying in a house across the street, and I'd walked over to see if I could find someone to do my laundry. Standing on the front steps was a middle-aged Englishman. He introduced himself as Richard, a former member of the 22nd SAS. He had a rifle slung over his shoulder, and he was slobbering drunk. Hearing my accent, he immediately lit into Americans as fearful and weak. "Come with me, my Yankee Doodle Dandy wanker," he said. "I'll take you places you've never been."

Like where? I said. He looked as if he were about to tell me. Then he stopped and lurched forward, almost on top of me. "You're not Irish, are you?" he demanded, breathing in my face. Nope. "Good man!" He all but embraced me. He'd killed enough of the Irish in Ulster, he said. He'd hate to have to do it again.

About ten days after I left Iraq, Richard put three bullets into a man he was supposed to be protecting. Apparently, it was an accident. He'd forgotten to take his rifle off automatic and . . . well, you know. The man survived. Richard was fired. It turned out he had never served in the SAS.

It's hard to know how many Richards are working as contractors in Iraq. None work for Kelly McCann, which is one of the reasons DynCorp subcontracted his company to come to

Baghdad, to straighten out some of the messes created by the postwar hiring spree. McCann's company, a division of Kroll that specializes in high-end security, has only eighteen employees. All are extensively vetted. All, like their boss, are disciplined and superior, exactly the sort of people you'd want standing next to you if someone started shooting in your direction.

During the week that I was in Baghdad, Kelly and his men spent their time trying to secure the area around the Gardenia, an industrial neighborhood across the river from the Green Zone. In addition to being filled with Westerners, the hotel is just down the street from an Iraqi police station, a dangerous place to be. (At the time, police stations were being blown up or coming under fire daily in Baghdad.) The contractors had turned the entire street into what looked to me like a garrison.

There was a manned roadblock at one end, covered by gun positions on roofs above. The hotel garden was strung with netting to repel RPGs; its windows were covered with Mylar to reduce flying glass from bomb blasts. Teams of plainclothes security men patrolled the surrounding neighborhood at all times. Only approved delivery trucks were allowed on the street. When a building contractor wanted to deliver a load of bricks to a homeowner building an addition, guards accompanied the driver to the brickyard to make certain no explosives were added along the way. "I'm building my own Green Zone," said Chad Morman, the twenty-nine-year-old Georgian in charge of physical security around the Gardenia.

I liked Chad. Like many of the men who work for Kelly, he had a ferocious background—Marine close-quarters-combat instructor and amateur kickboxer—but a strikingly understated personal demeanor. He rarely raised his voice. He never boasted or talked about hurting people. If you ran into him at Home Depot, you'd never guess what he did for a living. One night after dinner, I accompanied him as he patrolled the area around the hotel.

The first thing I noticed was how popular Chad was with animals. Every twenty yards or so, a cat seemed to run from the bushes and brush against his trousers. This struck me as unusual, mostly because you don't see many pets in Iraq. Observant Muslims don't as a rule like dogs—Muhammad specifically condemned them—and the bias apparently extends to other small, furry domesticated animals. Along with divergent beliefs about toilet paper, this is part of the great cultural divide between Iraqis and their occupiers. Sometimes it is a source of tension. "Are people who don't like dogs even *worth* liberating?" I heard one American contractor wonder aloud.

I mentioned this to Chad. He told me that when he first arrived in Baghdad, his guards amused themselves by torturing stray cats, kicking them and pelting them with rocks. Chad put an end to this immediately. "I told them if they bothered the animals, I'd shoot them. I was sort of joking, but they believed me." Ever since, the guards had treated the cats like sacred objects, giving them wide berth and, when possible, shepherding them Chad's way. The cats apparently were grateful.

We were almost to the end of the street when we heard voices. It sounded like young men speaking in stage whispers, and it was, three of them. They emerged from the shadows directly in front of us. "Stop!" Chad yelled, pulling a .45 out of his leg holster. One of them kept coming, walking purposefully with a cigarette in his mouth. "Stop right there!" At about twenty-five feet, Chad leveled the gun at the man's chest. At fifteen feet, he pulled back the hammer. The man was about a foot from being killed when he finally stopped. Without lowering the gun, Chad motioned for the men to turn around. They did, and so did we. We were outnumbered and had only a handgun; there wasn't much to do but leave.

We returned to the post, and Chad told the guards what had happened. Go find out what those guys are doing there, he said. "If they live here, that's okay. If they don't, tell them to move the fuck on." The guards nodded eagerly and trotted off. "Wait!" yelled Chad. The guards stopped. "Don't shoot anybody unless somebody shoots at you." The guards nodded again. Chad turned to me. "You got to tell them that. If someone pisses them off, they're likely to open up."

The guards, like most DynCorp hires in Iraq, were Kurds from the north of the country. "They're more loyal," Chad explained. "Plus, they don't like people from Baghdad." This made them less likely to be co-opted by the locals. It also made them somewhat hotheaded.

A few minutes later, the guards returned with the three men. Chad was surprised. "There's the dude I pulled a gun on," he said. He hadn't expected to see the man and his friends again. The guards, meanwhile, were pleased with themselves. They deposited the prisoners in front of their boss with obvious pride, like a cat dropping a mouse on the kitchen floor. The three men looked confused and irritated.

Which made sense, since they lived in the neighborhood and, strictly speaking, hadn't been caught doing anything wrong. This all became clear fairly quickly. "If they live there, it's no problem," Chad said to a guard who was acting as the translator. "Tell them it's no problem. I just wanted to see what they were doing down there."

But it wasn't so simple. Apparently one of the men had an attitude problem. He'd been rude or mouthy or something less than grateful on the walk down the street. The guards were anxious to shoot him. One of them pulled Chad aside to ask permission. "No, no, no," Chad said, shaking his head. The guard looked disappointed. "Any time," he said in heavily accented English. "Any time." He meant it.

A little before midnight, I went up to the roof to call my wife from a satellite phone. About a minute into the conversation, I heard gunshots. They sounded close. I tried to ignore them. They got louder, closer. The shots were coming from two or three directions. There were several AK-47s and at least one pistol. Someone was firing very near our house.

Actually, at it. I'd heard people talk about the funny cracking noise that bullets make when they pass close over your head. It took me a moment to realize that was the sound I was hearing. I sat down. "What *is* that?" said my wife, who was on a tree-lined street six thousand miles away, driving the kids home from school. "Nothing," I was about to say, when the door to the roof opened and an Iraqi man with a rifle ran out toward me.

It was one of Chad's guards. He was squinting, trying to adjust his eyes to the darkness. He looked agitated. Suddenly, I could see what was about to happen. He'd spot me squatting in the shadows, panic, and shoot. I'd die on a roof in Baghdad, killed by one of the most pro-American Iraqis in the city. All while talking to my wife. It wouldn't be a noble death.

"It's me!" I yelled. "American!" The guard lowered his rifle. I got off the phone and ran downstairs to my bedroom. The hall and stairway reeked of cordite. Outside, the firing had intensified. The noise sounded different from usual. It wasn't the typical fully automatic fire, sustained and essentially uncontrolled. (Arabs have a well-deserved reputation for "spray and pray" marksmanship.) The shots were coming in short bursts. Someone was aiming. I took this as an ominous sign.

Kelly had gone to bed an hour before and was just waking up when I came in. I filled him in on the gunfight as casually as I could. He seemed interested but not worried. He became more concerned when Chad burst in. Chad was breathing hard. He had just come from outside, where several firefights were going on. "They're closing in on us," he said.

The hair on the back of my neck went up. I pictured men in checkered kaffiyehs charging up the stairs with guns, a final desperate shoot-out. Kelly turned to me. "Put on your vest," he said. I threw the armor plates over my head, fumbling with the Velcro straps. I grabbed my gun and went out into the hallway, trying to remember to stay away from the windows. Kelly and Bill Frost joined me, and we headed up to the roof.

By the time we got there, whoever was laying siege to our house (two different groups of men, we later learned) was being chased off by return fire. Kelly looked around for a minute, then went back to bed. Bill and I stayed up for another hour talking with Chad on the roof. Bill had spent months in Somalia around the time of the Black Hawk disaster in 1993, commanding a surveillance team in downtown Mogadishu. Feuding warlords, khat-addled lunatics driving pickups with .50-caliber machine guns mounted on the back—it sounded like a hairy place. Bill said Baghdad was more dangerous.

As he spoke, he leaned over the side of the building, scanning the street below and thinking about how he'd attack the compound if he were an Iraqi insurgent. Wouldn't be hard, he concluded. "Fifteen guys with RPGs could lay waste to this place." (The next day, Bill announced plans to put a new gun emplacement on top of the apartment building across the street. "We're going to tell the people who live there. They can eat a cold bowl of fuck if they don't like it.")

Finally the adrenaline subsided and I headed off to sleep. As I was walking across the roof, another firefight broke out in the neighborhood, this one a few blocks away. Bill and Chad ignored it. The hallway still smelled of cordite when I got downstairs.

It wasn't until I was flat on my back that the strangest part of the night sank in: no one outside our immediate compound had seemed to notice the firefight. The gunfire had gone on for fifteen minutes. The noise had been tremendous and un-mistakable. Yet nobody—not U.S. soldiers, not cops from the Iraqi police station 150 yards away, not representatives of the famously benevolent "international community," whoever they might be—had come by to ask what happened, who did it, or if anyone was hurt. There were no authorities to call. No one cared. We were totally alone.

Not as alone as the rest of the people in the neighborhood, however. We were on a residential street. Iraqi families lived on both sides of us. What did they think? Hundreds of rounds had been fired—hundreds of needle-tipped, copper-jacketed missiles whipping through the neighborhood at half a mile a second. What happened to them all? Where did the bullets go? Into parked cars and generators and water tanks. Into people's living rooms and kitchens and bedrooms, and sometimes into human flesh.

It must have been terrifying to live nearby, or to live any-where in Baghdad. You couldn't blame the coalition forces ex-actly. They weren't doing most of the shooting. But they didn't seem to be doing much about it, either. On the street where I was staying, they weren't doing anything. And how could they? All the foreign troops in Iraq hadn't been able to keep the coun-try's main airport safe enough to use. A single block in Baghdad wasn't going to get their attention. By necessity, it was left to civilian contractors, or whoever else had the time, energy, and firearms to police their own tiny sections of Iraq.

The Coalition Provisional Authority that now runs Iraq has been half explicit about this. The CPA has acknowledged that civilians must carry weapons by establishing rules about what sorts of weapons they can carry (small arms only—no grenades, .50 calibers, or RPGs). It also freely issues photo-ID weapons permits. But the authority has made no provisions for legitimately purchasing guns and ammunition. A contractor working in Iraq has to have firearms, but he can't buy any from the U.S. military. Nor can he easily ship his own into the country from the United States. His only practical option is to find guns on the local black market—"Our own personal gun buyback program," as Bill put it.

One afternoon, Jack Altizer invited me to see the DynCorp armory, located in a storeroom in the basement of the Baghdad Hotel. The room, about twenty feet square, was stacked floor to ceiling with weapons. There were foot lockers full of AK-47s, dozens of crates of ammunition, shelves sagging with every sort of exotic weapon: a Thompson submachine gun from the 1930s, a World War II–vintage Soviet burp gun, Mausers, Walthers, guns so old and weird they were hard to identify. On a table in the middle of the room were more than a dozen 9mm pistols, each with "Gift from Saddam" stamped in Arabic on the barrel. In the corner were two leather shotgun cases. They had once held 12-gauge side-by-sides, custom fitted in Paris. Both were monogrammed S.H. They came from one of the presidential palaces.

Where did you get all this? I asked. Jack grinned. "I got here when there was still looting. We decided to join in." In fact, he had little choice but to join in. He needed guns for his men, and there was no other way to get them. At the time, there was so much weaponry floating around Iraq, no one knew what to do with it. At one point, a U.S. soldier offered to give Jack a million and a half AK-47 rounds. Logistics prevented him from accepting. "I couldn't carry it to my room," he said.

It's not hard to find guns in Iraq. But once a contractor gets them, he receives virtually no instructions from the U.S. government on when and how he is allowed to use them. The only firm guideline so far has come from chief administrator Paul Bremer himself. At a meeting with contractors in the Green Zone last fall, Bremer conceded that civilians in Iraq could have to protect themselves because the CPA could not guarantee anyone's safety. His one request: identify your target before you engage—know whom you're shooting at.

This level of ambiguity makes many contractors nervous. As former soldiers, they prefer clear rules of engagement. What if they kill someone? Worse, what if they kill the wrong person? Neither would be unusual in a place like Iraq. Then what? If a U.S. soldier shoots someone under murky circumstances, the Army's Criminal Investigation Division looks into it. But the CID has no authority over civilians off base. "I don't even know that if you engage someone there's even an investigative authority to follow up," Kelly said. "With no parameters, how do I know if I've done something wrong? It's like the Wild West, but nobody's the sheriff."

Or, depending on how you look at it, everybody is. Last summer, a British contractor was run off the road by bandits on a highway south of Baghdad. The contractor, a former SAS man, got out of his car and pretended to surrender. When the bandits approached, he shot both of them. One didn't die immediately, so he clubbed him to death. The Brit was still laughing about it when Bill ran into him a week later.

Not all contractors want more CPA oversight of their activities. That's understandable. There's something to be said for limited bureaucratic interference. One night in December, two DynCorp contractors caught a man they'd been looking for outside the Baghdad Hotel. According to local witnesses, the man had kidnapped several children and attempted to sell them. The contractors reduced him to a bloody mound before turning "what was left of him" over to the Iraqi police. They told me about it at breakfast the next morning. They looked pleased.

Of course, contractors aren't always high-minded. With no one watching, it's tempting to settle scores. The week before I arrived, Sean Penn came to Iraq on some sort of special assignment for the *San Francisco Chronicle*. The actor was getting out of a cab in downtown Baghdad when a group of contractors spotted him. The contractors didn't share Penn's politics. Plus, they found the idea of him annoying. So they took his camera and made him stand in the rain for forty-five minutes while they ran an imaginary security check on his equipment. There was nothing Penn could do about it. They had guns. He didn't. Tough luck.

Kelly told me that the maximum he allowed any of his men to stay in Iraq without a vacation was three months. Unlike the military, contractors work in relatively isolated conditions, without the security and support of hundreds of their peers. In this environment, the ambient threat—the constant, sometimes sublimated, but always present knowledge that you could get killed—can get to a person quickly. People get twitchy. I was beginning to feel it after just a week.

It started one morning while we were driving through a traffic circle downtown, on our way from the Gardenia to the Baghdad Hotel. An Iraqi man in a Crown Victoria turned his car around in the middle of the circle and came after us, trying to T-bone our SUV. Bill, who was driving, whipped onto a side street, then pulled a high-speed U-turn. The man in the Crown Vic was right behind, bearing down. There was no question now that he was trying to hit us. I was lying in the cargo area in the back of the Nissan, trying to get as flat as possible as Chad aimed his MP5 over my chest.

Suddenly Chad yelled, "Wait! There's a kid in the car." I looked up. He was right. In the passenger seat was a boy about six. The man, whoever he was, had a death grip on the wheel, obviously determined to commit some life-altering act. Bill swerved, then slammed on the brakes. The Crown Vic flew past.

I still don't know what that was all about, though there was violence in it. For some reason, more than anything, it made me want to leave Iraq.

We were planning to leave the next morning anyway. For the final twenty-four hours, I thought a lot about death. I'd thought about it some before leaving the United States, of course. I'd written out a will and letters to my wife and children. On the flight into Kuwait, Kelly and I talked about dying. "Everybody thinks it won't happen to them," he'd said. "But why not? It's going to happen to someone."

It had seemed like a good point then. The words penetrated deeper every day we were in Iraq. The thought was unavoidable. During the entire week, there was only a single sustained period when there wasn't gunfire and explosions in the background—when we had lunch with a Pentagon official on the fourth floor of the nearly deserted Baghdad airport. As Bill put it one morning at breakfast, grimly, "It's just a matter of time."

We left Baghdad at six thirty in the morning. Kelly was driving this time. He turned out to be as talented as Bill. On the highway out of the city, we squeezed between two tractor trailers at about 95 miles an hour. I could have reached out and touched either one with only my fingers protruding from the car. It was exciting as hell. I was going to miss driving in Iraq.

I was not going to miss Nasiriyah. The city has about as bad a vibe to it as any place I've ever been. Ten miles away, my skin began to crawl. The fact that our fuel tanks were almost empty added to the tension. We were driving slowly on the outskirts of town, caught in traffic. It was market day, and the road was lined with hundreds of people, most of them staring at us. Both gas stations we passed were closed. Someone nearby started firing a gun at us. Kelly pulled the SUV into the oncoming lane, and then back again. There were too many vehicles to go anywhere. We were boxed in.

A few tense minutes later, we came to a working gas station. It was packed with people, crowds of them, some waiting for gas, some just milling around outside a mosque next door. It was the worst possible place to stop, but there was no choice. We needed fuel. We initiated the gas-station takeover.

It was different this time. I hadn't thought about it till now, but we had fewer armed men with us than we'd had driving in. Kelly stayed with the car, which was left running in case we needed to leave quickly. I hopped out with my rifle to keep an eye on two large groups of men who seemed to be approaching us. I walked about twenty feet, then turned to my left to see what the man next to me was doing. That's when I realized there was nobody next to me, no one whose lead I could follow. I was by myself.

During our first conversation about going to Iraq, Kelly and I had talked about situations like this. It's one thing to believe in the principle of self-defense. Most people do. It's quite another to make the conscious decision to kill someone. Kelly had made it clear that I'd have to decide ahead of time whether I'd be willing. "Final confirmation of an attack usually comes in the form of injury to you," he'd said. "If you feel threatened, engage, up to and including lethal force." Survival means acting first. Hesitation equals death.

I'd had plenty of opportunities to mull this over since getting to Baghdad. I didn't want to hurt another person. The idea sickened me. But now I knew for certain that I would, without hesitation.

The groups of men were definitely walking toward me now, talking to one another and looking angry. The crowd behind them was getting larger and more agitated. In my peripheral vision I could see shapes, people darting in and out between cars parked in the gas line. I hoped someone else was watching them.

At the center of the group advancing on me were two young-ish men with tough-guy expressions on their faces. They were obviously leading whatever was about to happen. I decided to shoot them first. I'd start with the one on the right. I unfolded the AK's paratrooper stock and tucked it into my shoulder, rais-ing the muzzle. Then I switched off the safety. I waited for one of them to make a quick movement.

Neither one did. In fact, both stopped where they were and glared at me. I glared back. Five minutes later, our tanks were full and we left.

There was no firefight at the gas station, but I left feeling as if something important and horrible had just happened. I'd been forced to make a decision about life and death. There were no official guidelines. There was no one around to make the call but me, just as there would have been no one around to judge the consequences. I could have done anything. The only rules were those I imposed on myself. I hated it. It was an instructive experience. For a moment, I felt what it is to be an American civilian contractor in Iraq.

———

Back in 1998, it was still shocking to hear total strangers reveal the intimate details of their lives. The internet was young then; we didn't have Facebook. If you wanted to tell someone you'd never met about your secret plastic surgery or your sad tale of sexual dysfunction, you had to find an audience. You had to do it in person. A surprising number of people were willing to make the effort.

THE SELF-REVEALERS

Weekly Standard, June 15, 1998

A couple of years ago, I watched an entire infomercial about toupees. It was late, and I was stranded alone in a motel room, but it wasn't boredom that kept me tuned in. It was the testimonials. "The girls at the health club used to laugh at me," one satisfied wig buyer explained to the camera. "Not anymore." (Wait till they see this infomercial, I thought.) A half dozen other guys in bad rugs followed with their hard-luck tales of life before hair: "I couldn't get a date." "I was afraid to go shopping." "I was stuck in a dead-end job." In each case, a new hairpiece had been the answer. It made for compelling television.

But it also made me wonder: What was the point? Why go to the trouble and expense of pretending you're not bald, only to go on television and talk about your fake hair? It didn't make sense.

Until Viagra. The *Washington Post* broke news of the erectile miracle in a front-page story one Sunday in April. "It really, really works," enthused Alfred Pariser, a retired movie executive from Rancho Mirage, California. As if to prove it, the *Post* ran a photo of Pariser cuddling with his wife, Cheryl. In the picture, the Parisers look happy but worn out, and no wonder. Thanks to Viagra, Alfred told the paper, he and Cheryl are now mating "sometimes two or three times an evening."

Pariser may be exaggerating a bit—Viagra or not, he's fifty-eight years old—but that's hardly remarkable given the subject. What is remarkable is that he and his wife were willing to tell the world about their sex life. Why did they do it? Because, like the infomercial wig-wearers, the Parisers can't help themselves. They're compulsive self-revealers.

A lot of Americans are, I've learned. A couple of weeks ago I caught a cab in Los Angeles. We hadn't gone a mile before the driver launched into a monologue about all the unsavory people who have ridden in his car over the years: actors, drunken foreign businessmen, people who don't tip. The worst, he confided, are the politicians. "They're just the lowest," he said. "I mean, I cheat on my taxes, but those guys . . ."

It went on like this for half an hour, virtually every sentence revealing something new and embarrassing about the driver's personal life—how he'd once worked as a hash dealer in India; how his son, the one with the drug problem, had finally found happiness doing body piercing in Hawaii; how he himself still smoked pot from time to time, though increasingly he was turning to concentrated ginseng oil for a more natural high.

By the time we got to the hotel I was exhausted. "Here's my card," he said cheerfully, leaning over the seat. "Give me a call when you come back to town." Sure thing, chief. I'm being transferred to the IRS field office here next week. I'll look you up then.

That's what I should have said. Instead I just took his card and thanked him for the insights. It's hard to know what to say when you're in the company of a compulsive self-revealer. All you can do is listen.

And over the years I have: To the woman next to me on the plane who talked for an hour and a half about her husband's testicular cancer and subsequent nervous breakdown. To the car-service driver who explained how he was committing adultery with his next-door neighbor. (He gave me his card, too.) To the hitchhiker I picked up outside Baltimore who informed me that although he'd had some "problems" with schizophrenia in the past, his time in prison seemed to have eased the symptoms. And of course to countless tales of addiction, self-help, and recovery. Just the other day, a cabby spent the entire trip from Capitol Hill to Georgetown reading me selections from his unpublished poetry.

Self-revealers ought to be a reporter's dream. Who needs Deep Throat when the guy next to you in line at CVS can't wait to tell you about every appalling thing he's ever seen or done? It sounds great. I can't stand it.

Last fall, by weird coincidence, I wound up on the phone with a man who had been my soccer coach in the third grade. I was doing a story on a topic he knew something about, and before we got down to the point of the call, we chatted for a while. He mentioned his wife and children, whom I remembered well. Then, without warning, he began to compulsively reveal. "Here's an interesting story," he said. "A couple of years ago this banker friend of mine told me about this beautiful girl, absolutely gorgeous. He said, 'Why don't you try her? She's terrific. She's a hooker.' And I said, 'Okay, that sounds great.' So I went to her condominium one night and . . ."

My mouth hung open. Don't say it, I pleaded wordlessly. Please, don't say it.

But he did. Graphically. No doubt he felt better afterward. Talking to me was a lot easier than going to confession. At least for him.

———

*It feels a little strange at this point to include a long, lauda-
tory piece about Senator John McCain of Arizona. McCain
lived an undeniably remarkable life, but unfortunately, in
his final years, he disgraced himself with nastiness and dis-
honesty. Those qualities were always present in McCain.
They were obvious if you knew him, though in retrospect I
didn't pay enough attention to his dark side. But most of the
time, McCain's flashes of ugliness were more than offset by
his charm, energy, and good humor. From my perspective,
though, his best quality was his recklessness. Unlike most
politicians, McCain preferred to live extemporaneously,
making things up as he went along, itinerary included. He
loved unexpected surprises. McCain didn't fear what might
happen next, and he didn't care who watched. It was a kind
of performance art. Covering McCain as a candidate, you'd
wake up in one city without any real idea of where you
might end up at the end of the day. There will never be
another presidential campaign like John McCain's run in
2000. It was the last one. I'll always be grateful to McCain,
whatever his faults, for letting me see it.*

"ON THE ROAD"

Weekly Standard, March 27, 2000

Franklin, New Hampshire—January 30, 2000

It's Super Bowl Sunday and John McCain is sitting on his campaign bus finishing off the second of two hamburgers. McCain has just given a rousing speech to a packed VFW hall, and he's hungry. An aide has arrived with an appliance-sized cardboard box of McDonald's food. As McCain eats, dripping ketchup liberally on his tie, the aide tosses burgers over his head to the outstretched hands of reporters. One of the burgers comes close to beaning George "Bud" Day, a seventyish retired Air Force colonel who has been traveling with McCain. Around his neck Day wears the Congressional Medal of Honor, which he won for heroism during the years he spent with McCain in a North Vietnamese prison camp. "Where's the booze?" Day growls. Someone gestures to the back of the bus, and Day soon disappears to rejoin a group of fellow former POWs who, by the sound of it, have already located the bar.

"Senator," says a reporter who came on for the first time at the previous stop, "can I ask you a couple of questions?" McCain laughs. "We answer all questions on this bus. And sometimes we lie. Mike Murphy is one of the greatest liars anywhere." McCain points what's left of his hamburger at Murphy. "Aren't you, Mike?" Murphy, a thirty-seven-year-old political consultant who is both McCain's message guru and his comic foil, nods solemnly. "Murphy has spent his life trying to destroy people's political careers," McCain says. "I'll have yours done on Tuesday," Murphy replies.

The reporter looks a little confused, but goes ahead and asks his question, which is about McCain's strategy for winning the New Hampshire primary. Before McCain can answer, Murphy jumps in with an insult. "The problem with the media," he says, "is you're obsessed with process, with how many left-handed, Independent soccer moms are going to vote." McCain translates: "You're assholes, in other words," he says, chortling and grinning so wide you can see the gold in his molars. About this time, one of the POWs sticks his head into the compartment where McCain is sitting. Sounds of clinking glasses and raspy old-guy laughter follow him from the back of the bus. "We're picking your cabinet back there, John," he says.

It takes only a day or two of this sort of thing for the average political reporter to decide that John McCain is about the coolest guy who ever ran for president. A candidate who offers total access all the time, doesn't seem to use a script, and puts on a genuinely amusing show? If you're used to covering campaigns from behind a rope line—and virtually every reporter who doesn't cover McCain full time is—it's almost too good to believe. The Bush campaign complains that McCain's style and personality have caused many reporters to lose their objectivity about him. The Bush campaign is onto something.

There are reporters who call McCain "John," sometimes even to his face and in public. And then there are the employees of major news organizations who, usually at night in the hotel bar, slip into the habit of referring to the McCain campaign as "we"—as in, "I hope we kill Bush."

Nashua, New Hampshire—February 1

Primary day has arrived, and the final distinctions between McCain's mobile primary campaign and your average sophomore road trip to Vegas are breaking down. By 8 a.m., the last of the coffee, bottled water, Diet Coke, and candy have disappeared from the bus. All that remains is beer and donuts. McCain is eating the donuts. He's in a sentimental mood. Late polls have shown him likely to beat Bush today, but he doesn't seem particularly jubilant about it. Instead McCain mentions three times how much he will miss rolling through New Hampshire in a bus. He seems to mean it. With McCain you get the feeling that the pleasure is in the process—that he considers the actual election a signal that the fun part is over. "It's been the great experience of my life," he says. "I'm feeling a little wistful."

McCain returns to his hotel suite and spends most of the

afternoon chatting with his POW friends. At seven the networks declare him the winner. The room erupts in cheers. All except McCain, who stands by himself, arms folded in front of him, unsmiling and not saying a word.

After his speech a few hours later, McCain and his wife are hustled into a conference room in the hotel for their first round of post-victory television interviews. Outside, the scene in the lobby looks like the end stages of a particularly rowdy wedding reception. The campaign has hired a couple of heavily tattooed Manhattan nightclub DJs to run the sound and lights. One of them—the guy with five earrings and control of the CD player—recently came off tour with the Foo Fighters and Nine Inch Nails. He's blasting a tune by Fatboy Slim. Hundreds of people are dancing and cheering and yelling.

Inside, where McCain is, the room is dark and still. Cameramen and sound technicians are fiddling with coils of wires on the floor. A photographer, exhausted from days on the road, has taken off his boots and is lying flat on his back asleep surrounded by camera bags. A CNN crew works to dial up the satellite link to *Larry King Live*.

McCain seems oblivious to it all. He has his eyes locked, unblinking, on the blank camera in front of him. His teeth are set, his chin thrust forward in go-ahead-I-dare-you position. Between interviews, he maintains the pose. McCain looks on edge and unhappy, not at all like a man who has just achieved the greatest political triumph of his life. There is no relief on his face.

It's a dramatic change from a week or two before. Back then, before he had seriously considered the possibility that he could become president, McCain seemed determined to run the most amusing and least conventional campaign possible. His style became more free-form by the moment. In the final days before the New Hampshire primary, McCain took to pulling wackos out of the crowd at his town meetings and giving them air time. "Anyone who makes the effort to show up in costume deserves the microphone," McCain explained when a reporter asked what he was doing. At one point he handed the mike to a man dressed like a shark. A few days later he turned the stage over to a guy with a boot on his head and a pair of swim fins glued to his shoulders like epaulets.

For a politician it was risky, almost lunatic behavior—imagine if the shark man had started raving about Satanism, or the pleasures of child pornography. McCain appeared to thrive on it. Now, sitting in the dark waiting for Larry King, he seems burdened, or at least bewildered. Something unexpected has happened to John McCain: He won. He is the dog who caught the car.

It's close to midnight when the staff bus leaves the hotel for the Manchester airport. There's a case of champagne on the floor near the driver, but everyone is drinking beer. The whole thing is so amusingly improbable—the joke that came true. A few minutes later, Mike Murphy scans the AP wire and learns that McCain's lead has grown to 19 points. He chuckles. "What a caper," he says.

The bus finally pulls onto the tarmac and comes to a stop beside an elderly-looking jet with Pan Am markings. Representative Lindsey Graham of South Carolina, who has spent all week stumping for McCain, peers out the window and spots it. He looks slightly concerned. I think I can tell what he's thinking: Didn't Pan Am go out of business years ago? "What kind of plane is that?" he asks Murphy. "It's a Russian copy of a 727," Murphy says. "It was decommissioned from Air Flug in the 70s. The Bulgarian mechanics checked it out and said it runs fine. We're not wasting precious campaign dollars on expensive American-made, quality aircraft. A minivan full of vodka and a sack of potatoes and we got it for the whole week."

Murphy seems to be joking, though over the next month, as the campaign travels from coast to coast and back again and again, the plane does take on a certain Eastern European feel. The flight attendants speak in hard-to-pin-down foreign accents. The paint around the entryway is peeling. The bathrooms are scarred with cigarette burns. The right engine periodically makes loud, unexplained thumping noises. Occasionally, in flight, the plane lists dramatically to one side for no apparent reason. Almost every landing ends with at least three bounces along the runway. As the plane touches down at a private airstrip in rural Ohio one afternoon, a voice comes over the intercom with a disconcerting announcement: "Ladies and gentlemen, welcome to Indianapolis."

None of this bothers McCain, who has successfully bailed out of four airplanes and knows he's not going to die in one. (Nervous reporters joke that if the plane does start to go down, everyone on board will try to hop into his lap.) He spends most of his time in the air asleep. Presidential candidates traditionally sit at the front of the plane, behind a curtain where they can confer privately with their staffs. McCain does very little in private. After each event he reboards the plane like any other commuter, opens and closes a series of overhead bins in search of a place to store his coat, then finds a seat in economy class and sprawls out, head back and mouth open. Before long he is snoring quietly.

If it's after four in the afternoon, just about everyone else has a drink. Cocktails are a recurring motif on the McCain campaign. The candidate himself rarely drinks more than a single chilled vodka, and then only in private. Members of his staff are almost always in the bar till closing. (When the bar at the Copley Plaza in Boston finally stopped serving one night, one of the campaign's traveling press secretaries went to his room, emptied the contents of the minibar into a pillow case, and returned to keep the festivities going.) At the front of the plane, right outside the cockpit and across from the cigarette-burned lavatory, are coolers of beer and wine, surrounded by baskets of candy bars and plates of cheese cubes. At the back is a bar—not a rack of miniature airplane bottles, but a table laid out with quarts of booze, ice, and mixers. Minutes after takeoff a crowd gathers near the rear galley.

A cable news producer works to wrench the cap off a beer bottle with a cigarette lighter as a group of cameramen sit nearby chatting and drinking horrible airplane champagne out of two-piece plastic cups. John Weaver, McCain's taciturn political director, stands at the bar pouring himself an unusually large drink. In the row next to him is the campaign's advance team, which is busy stuffing confetti guns—thick plastic pipes with CO_2 canisters at the bottom—with orange streamers in preparation for the next rally. They're drinking, too. Cindy McCain, the candidate's wife, approaches, a glass of wine in hand, only to be intercepted by an MTV correspondent who looks about fifteen. "Could I get a quick interview?" asks the MTV girl. "Sure," says Cindy. Sitting off to the side, watching it all, is Greg Price, the guy who will drive the bus when the plane lands.

Price has been with McCain since the beginning of the New Hampshire campaign, when he was hired from a charter bus company in Ohio. He is thirty, a laid-back, chain-smoking Navy veteran with no previous interest in politics. Price initially expected to be back home within a couple of weeks. That was in August. In December, he returned to Columbus briefly, got married, then left to rejoin McCain two days later. He has seen his wife for a total of twenty-four hours since. She is seven months pregnant. The New Hampshire primary changed Price's life.

Like a lot of former fighter pilots, John McCain is superstitious. He wears lucky shoes, eats lucky food, makes certain to get out on the correct side of the bed. His pockets are filled with talismans, including a flattened penny, a compass, a feather, and a pouch of sacred stones given to him by an Indian tribe in Arizona. He jokes about all of this, but he's not really kidding. At some point, McCain began to suspect that Price was a lucky bus driver. The campaign's rising poll numbers seemed to bolster this theory; the subsequent 19-point New Hampshire blowout proved it.

In the weeks since, Price has gone everywhere with McCain. Campaigns typically hire new bus drivers in each city. Those who travel stay in inexpensive hotels near the rest of the campaign staff. Price has stayed in McCain's hotel every night, sometimes in a suite. On some trips he has been a passenger rather than a driver. He has come to know McCain's family; on the night of the Arizona and Michigan primaries he sipped cocktails in the candidate's living room in Phoenix. ("You're never going home again," Cindy McCain told him when CNN announced that her husband had won both states.) And despite a long night at the bar in the Dearborn Hyatt, he is at the wheel of the bus at 8 a.m. Sunday morning to take McCain over to *Meet the Press*.

Detroit, Michigan—February 20

McCain lost the South Carolina primary last night, but you'd never know it from the way he's acting. He's in a great mood. As the bus rolls past miles of rubble-strewn vacant lots on the way to the television studio, McCain is laughing and telling story after story—about the late representative Mo Udall, about the Naval Academy, about the time he watched an Indian woman give birth in the corner of a bar in New Mexico. He doesn't seem upset about South Carolina. He hasn't come up with any talking points to explain his loss there. He doesn't appear to be preparing for *Meet the Press* in any way. McCain's aides aren't even sure how long he's going to be on the show this morning.

Half an hour? Fifteen minutes? No one seems to know. (The full hour, McCain discovers when he gets to the studio.) It's obvious that no one really cares, least of all McCain.

McCain has never had a reputation as much of a detail guy. He can do a pretty good campaign-finance-reform rap. He can talk forever about the need to open up Reagan National Airport to long-haul flights to the West Coast. He seems to know everything about American Indian tribes in Arizona. Venture far beyond those topics and the fine print gets blurry. As he explained one morning a few weeks ago, there's no reason to get sucked into "Talmudian" debates over policy. "I won't bother you with the details," McCain often says when a member of the audience at one of his speeches asks about a specific piece of legislation. "That's a very good question," he'll respond, and then neglect to answer it.

It's an effective technique on the stump. Most people don't really want to know the details. But it is also a reflection of the candidate's personality. McCain can be kind of reckless. In fact, he enjoys being kind of reckless, and so does his staff.

Not surprisingly, McCain is having a pretty rough time on *Meet the Press*. One of his most prominent supporters in South Carolina, it turns out, is affiliated with a magazine that has been hostile to the organized civil rights movement. Tim Russert is hammering McCain on the subject. McCain looks like he isn't sure what to say. In the next room, McCain's aides are watching the show by remote. John Weaver is eating a piece of melon and chuckling about the campaign's unofficial slogan, "Burn It Down." "It's like Stokely Carmichael," Weaver says. "Power to

the people!" He throws his fist into the air. "Burn it down—
I love that." A few days later, at the bar on the plane, Weaver
comes up with a new slogan: "Eradicate Evil." "We're going to
have T-shirts printed," Weaver says. "They're going to have 'E²'
above crossed light sabers."

Saginaw, Michigan—February 21

McCain seems to be taking his own slogans to heart. At a rally
this morning in Traverse City, he spent more time than usual
beating up on the Republican Party. "My friends," he said
gravely, "my party has lost its way. My party has become captive to special interests." In conversations with reporters, he has
begun to make disparaging references to the "Christian right,"
the "extreme right," and the "bunch of idiots" who run Bob
Jones University. On the bus from Saginaw to Ypsilanti, he goes
all the way, recalling with a smile "that old bumper sticker: The
Christian Right Is Neither."

Part of this is calculated rhetoric: McCain knows most
evangelicals aren't planning to vote for him anyway. Bashing
them might bring him more votes from moderates. But part of
it is heartfelt. During the race in South Carolina, leaflets were
distributed at political events that savaged Cindy McCain for
her early-nineties addiction to prescription painkillers. McCain
blames conservative Christian groups (and to some extent, the
Bush campaign) for the flyers, as well as for a series of ugly push
polls. For the first time, he talks about his opponents in a way
that seems bitter. "They're going around saying Cindy's a drug

addict who's not fit to be in the White House," McCain says, his fists clenched. "What am I supposed to do? Come out and make a statement that my wife is not a drug addict?"

St. Louis, Missouri—March 2

He is still mulling the question a couple of weeks later when the campaign plane touches down in St. Louis. McCain is in town for a few hours to participate by remote in a televised forum with Bush and Alan Keyes. It is the last scheduled debate. McCain knows he must do well. He and half a dozen advisers gather in the conference room of a television station downtown to eat barbecue and prepare. McCain is resigned to appearing tonight with Alan Keyes ("If we tried to keep him out of the debate, he might chain himself to my front door"), but it is clear that the very thought of George W. Bush makes him agitated. McCain is angry at Bush. Very angry.

I happen to be standing next to the coffeemaker when McCain walks over to pour his ninth cup of the day. He's thinking about what he needs to do in the debate, and about mistakes he has made in weeks past. "I've got to try not to get down into the weeds tonight," he says, to himself as much as to me. Bush may be a dishonest candidate running a vicious campaign, but in the end . . . McCain looks up from his coffee. "Nobody gives a shit."

It's a good point, and absolutely true. Voters say they dislike attacks ads, but they generally believe them. They may feel sorry for a candidate who is being bashed over the head, but they tend to assume he must have done something wrong. And no matter how they feel about the accuracy of an attack, voters almost always perceive complaints about negative campaigning as whining. McCain knows all this. He also knows that the public doesn't believe that his campaign has behaved any more honorably than Bush's—particularly after McCain was caught lying last month about calls his campaign was making to voters in Michigan. Still, he is finding it hard to choke back how he feels. And how he feels is aggrieved.

McCain feels aggrieved fairly often, but for some reason his aides hate to admit it. One morning in New Hampshire, a reporter asked McCain what he would do if his fifteen-year-old daughter Meghan were raped and became pregnant. Would he allow her to have an abortion? McCain's face reddened as he listened to the question. After a family discussion, he replied slowly, "the final decision would be made by Meghan." Reporters pounced. But isn't that a pro-choice position? No, it's not, barked McCain. He looked furious.

Except he wasn't, it was explained later. Moments after McCain got off the bus, Todd Harris, the campaign's traveling press secretary, loped to the back where half a dozen reporters were still sitting, replaying their tapes and checking their notes. Harris had heard that someone, probably a wire-service reporter, was planning to describe McCain's response to the pro-choice question as "angry." Harris was determined to stop the adjective in its tracks. "Who's calling him 'angry'?" he demanded. No one confessed. McCain wasn't angry at all, Harris explained. He was merely "tense."

An hour and a half later, McCain's mood was upgraded.

A friend and I were sitting in a diner in downtown Manchester having breakfast when Todd Harris walked up to our booth carrying a statement from McCain on the abortion question. "I misspoke," it began, and went on to explain that if Meghan McCain were to get pregnant, the entire family, not Meghan alone, would decide what to do next. Dutifully retrieving our notebooks, my friend and I took this down. What about McCain's state of mind on the bus this morning? I asked. If he wasn't angry, is it fair to say he was irritated? That's acceptable, said Harris, nodding. "The AP's going with 'irritated.'"

With three minutes to go before air time in St. Louis, McCain is standing in the makeup room with a small group of advisers practicing his final comments. Rick Davis, his campaign manager, is humming "Ode to Joy" and pacing in the corner. McCain is using a thick blue marker to jot down some final revisions on a piece of scrap paper. His arm hooks in the shape of a sickle when he writes. His script is terrible. Looking out across an imaginary audience, McCain tries to recite what he has written. "I am a proud Reagan conservative," he says. "I am . . ." He stumbles, stops, then closes his eyes. For an instant he looks defeated, like he may not be able to continue. "I'm drawing a blank," he says. Mike Murphy leans forward until he is inches from McCain's face. "It's okay," he says softly.

And in seconds, it is. Soothing McCain is a large part of Murphy's job. McCain loves funny stories, and during lulls in the conversation on the bus he often asks Murphy to tell the one about the candidate he worked for who seemed to have Alzheimer's. Or about the campaign ad he claims he once made that accused an opponent of selling liquor to children. As Murphy tells the story, no matter how old it is, McCain breaks into hysterical, chair-pounding, hard-to-breathe laughter. McCain is genuinely amused by Murphy—he calls him "Murphistopheles," "The Swami," or simply "008," James Bond's little-known political consultant brother—but he is also calmed by his presence. A minute later, McCain grabs a final cup of coffee and heads into the studio.

The debate goes fairly smoothly for McCain, despite the obvious disadvantage of appearing by remote. Afterward, as he sits in a chair having his makeup removed, Murphy renders the verdict. "You were better than last time," he says. "You were good." "Do you think so?" asks McCain. It's not a rhetorical question. McCain honestly wants to know. "You were better and he was better," replies Murphy, "so it was sort of a blur."

San Jose, California—March 5

It soon becomes clear that a blur was not good enough. Two days before the California primary, it is obvious to virtually everyone that McCain will not win the nomination. His poll numbers have stopped rising. On the bus McCain seems, by turns, happier and more frustrated than ever. He is probably both. McCain prefers a righteous fight to almost anything, and Bush has given him new reason for outrage. A pair of rich Bush supporters in Texas have paid for an ad that attacks McCain's record on environmental issues. The ad is nasty and misleading, but what really incenses McCain is the idea of it. Billionaire Texans attacking my integrity? Outrageous. McCain gets hotter with every campaign stop.

"Tell Governor Bush to tell his cronies in Texas to stop destroying the American political system!" he shouts to a crowd in Ohio the Sunday before the primary. "If they get away with it," McCain tells reporters on the bus in California that night, "then I think it will change the nature of American politics forever. It will destroy it." The following morning, Bush's Texas cronies have become "Governor Bush's sleazy Texas buddies." By afternoon, McCain is accusing Bush and his supporters of trying "to steal this election." Stopping them, he says, "is a race against time." Finally, on what turns out to be one of the campaign's final bus rides, from LAX to the hotel, McCain's rhetoric reaches the boiling point. "If this is allowed to go unchecked," he says, "there's never going to be another young American who's ever going to vote again, over time."

McCain sounded about as angry as a presidential candidate can, or for that matter ever has. Except that in real life, he didn't. McCain is one of those people who have to be seen to be properly understood. On paper he can come off as a red-faced blowhard. In person the effect is far more complicated. McCain can accuse a person of subverting democracy and grin as he says it, all without being phony or disingenuous. He can rant about the evils of the special interests as he cheerfully attempts to eat an éclair with a plastic spoon. I've seen him do it. John McCain is a happy warrior, maybe the only real one in American politics.

Los Angeles, California—March 6

With defeat a day away, McCain is becoming even looser. He no longer seems mad about losing. He seems to feel vindicated. To McCain, a loss to the massive Bush machine is proof that everything he has been saying for the past year is true: that money is the decisive factor in politics. That the system is rigged to exclude outsiders and mavericks. That the Establishment felt so threatened by his honesty that it mobilized to crush him. Most of all, McCain considers his defeat evidence that he ran an honorable campaign—he lost because he would not do anything to win.

In speeches, he continues to swing wildly at Bush. On the bus, his jokes are getting more outrageous. ("We ought to call this The Bullshit Express," he says to Murphy. "Get someone to paint 1-800-BULLSHIT on the side.") Members of his staff are taking pictures of each other, presumably to capture a moment that is about to end. There is no longer much reason to pretend. Or for that matter to be polite about the opponent. Murphy has taken to wearing a pin that says "W stands for Wuss."

Beverly Hills, California—March 7

By quarter to eight on the night of the California primary, John McCain's presidential campaign has minutes to live. Tim Russert has just told McCain's guys that the latest round of exit polls from California looks bad. McCain is going to lose. He has already lost New York and Ohio and a couple of other states.

The networks haven't called the race yet, but the official pronouncement is imminent. McCain isn't one to drag things out. "All right, Johnny," he says, looking around the Beverly Hilton Hotel suite for John Weaver, the campaign's political director. It is Weaver's job to arrange concession calls to the Bush campaign. Weaver hates doing it, and for the moment he has disappeared.

"Johnny," McCain calls again.

Weaver's voice floats out of an adjoining bedroom. "Do I have to?" he asks. "Yep," says McCain.

A few minutes later, Weaver appears with a cell phone. His mouth is puckered, like he just took a shot of something sour. Bush is on the line. McCain takes the phone without hesitating. Then he leans back in his chair, feet on the coffee table in front of him, chilled vodka in hand, and congratulates the man he has come to despise. "My best to your family," McCain says. The conversation is over in less than thirty seconds.

And that's it—the end of John McCain's run for president. Now it's time to face the reporters waiting in the lobby, and from there on to the concession speech. For a moment the room is silent. A few of McCain's aides look like they might cry. Not McCain. He is buzzing with energy. "Let's go," he says, bouncing out of his chair. "Onward."

The last piece in this collection is the saddest, at least for me. It's a poignant experience returning from the place you love most. For my family that place has always been rural western Maine. The end of summer there always feels like a premonition of death. For the flowers and the leaves of northern New England, that's exactly what it is. They'll be gone soon. I always wonder if they know it. Once back home in Washington, I usually try to put thoughts like that away for the year, smothering them with work. But one fall, I did my best to capture the feeling.

ONE MAN'S TREASURE

Weekly Standard, October 2, 2000

S ummer houses are like time capsules. I remember this every June when we go to Maine, to the same place I've gone most of my life. My wife has been going with me every summer since we were in the tenth grade, so it always feels a bit like waking up back in high school when we arrive. In a dresser upstairs there are T-shirts I haven't worn since I took algebra. There are old letters in desks, matchbooks on the mantel from long-defunct restaurants, condiments in the kitchen I'm positive I recall from early childhood. At the bottom of the wood bin are newspapers announcing the crash of the *Challenger*.

This year my wife and I went determined to clean house. One of the first things we found was an answering machine, the outdated kind with the cassette tape and fake wood veneer. Before throwing it away, I played it. There were messages from people I hadn't called back since the Reagan administration. My own voice sounded about nineteen, which is how old I must have been when I recorded it. It was jarring. I decided to halt the archaeology expedition.

But there turned out to be no escaping unexpected reminders of the passage of time. One afternoon I was wandering around the boathouse looking for something when I found a small pyramid of old Coke bottles arranged on a rafter beam. Must be the kids' bottle collection, I thought to myself. And, I realized a moment later, it was. But not my kids—my parents' kids. These were bottles my brother and I had collected when we were little. Just where we'd left them.

Time seems to move especially fast in Maine, because our routine rarely changes when we're there. In the morning we build sand castles and throw sticks in the water for the dogs. In the afternoon we go swimming. The water is pretty chilly, so the kids usually climb out after a few minutes. They sit on the dock wrapped in towels shivering and watch me go "diving."

That's what they call it anyway. The reality is less impressive. I strap on a bright red children's swim mask (once part of a $9.99 "Junior Frogman" set from CVS) and swim around underwater. I must look preposterously dorky. But there's no one around to see it but the kids, and they're too young to be very judgmental about appearances. Plus, they're excited. There's always the chance I'll bring up treasures.

And sometimes I do. Thanks to careless ice fishermen and generations of clumsy people getting in and out of boats, there are quite a few man-made objects on the bottom. One year we found a tackle box that had tumbled unopened out of someone's canoe. This summer I pulled up an ancient-looking bottle with the word "Kaylene-Ol" (whatever that is) embossed on the side. But most of the time what I bring up is just junk: bricks, oarlocks, lost moorings, broken fishing lures, weirdly shaped rocks, unidentifiable hunks of rusted metal, an outboard prop or two, and lots and lots of freshwater oysters.

I throw it all piece by piece onto the dock while the kids yell happily. The stuff is usually gnarled and blackened and covered with moss, but that doesn't diminish its value. They split the loot into even piles and paw through it lovingly, like pieces of eight.

By August this year, the treasure piles had grown too large for the back porch. I cleaned off a shelf in the shed, displacing a decade's worth of mismatched plumbing supplies, hung a board across it with some old strap hinges, and called it a treasure chest. The kids put their cherished objects inside. They came back to check on them six or seven times a day every day until we went home.

And we finally did go home. We spent our last day in Maine as we always do, cleaning and closing up. I came to the shed last. I was about to lock the door when I noticed the shelf with the board across it. Suddenly I felt emotional. Next year, I thought, this place will look exactly the same, because it never changes. But we do. When we come back, the bricks and rocks and hunks of rusted metal will still be here, just where the children left them. I wonder if they'll still consider it treasure.

CONCLUSION

It's both the payoff and the tragedy of collecting a lifetime's worth of journalism that you get to see how the story ended. I wrote the piece about summer in Maine more than two decades ago, when my children were small. I remember that I had tears in my eyes when I finished the last paragraph. Will they still consider it treasure? I knew the answer even as I asked it. Those rusted hunks of metal sit to this day on the shelves of our shed by the water, but they're long ignored and forgotten. No one considers them treasure now. They never were. The real treasure was the moment, and I remember that like yesterday.

Thankfully, I remember a lot of happy moments from the past thirty years. Many of them have been preserved in the yellowing magazine stories about dead and irrelevant people that make up this book. Reading them now, I realize how much has changed, and forever. The world this book describes is mostly gone. That was fast. There's no use crying about that. We can't control it. We can only remember what we saw.

277